GRADE 8

SpringBoard®

Writing

Workshop with Grammar Activities

 CALIFORNIA EDITION

Acknowledgments

The College Board gratefully acknowledges the contributions of the following classroom teachers and writers who contributed to the creation of these writing workshops and grammar activities.

Lance Balla
K-12 English Curriculum Developer
Bellevue School District 405
Bellevue, Washington

Robert J. Caughey
AP English Teacher
San Dieguito Union High School District
San Diego, California

Charise Hallberg
English Language Arts AP Teacher
Bellevue School District 405
Bellevue, Washington

T. J. Hanify
English Language Arts AP Teacher
Bellevue School District 405
Bellevue, Washington

Susan Van Doren
English Language Arts & AP Teacher
Douglas County School District
Minden, Nevada

Michelle Lewis
Curriculum Coordinator: English
and Social Studies
Spokane Public School
Spokane, Washington

SpringBoard English Language Arts Staff

Joely Negedly
Senior Director
English and Social Studies Curriculum

JoEllen Victoreen
English Language Arts
Instructional Manager

Spencer Goncalves
Assistant ELA Editor

Doug Waugh
Executive Director
Product Management

Jennifer Duva
English Language Arts Editor

ISBN: 978-1-4573-0690-7

Contents

WRITING WORKSHOP

Writing Workshop 1 – The Writing Process: Strategies for Writing ...1

Writing Workshop 2 – Argumentative Writing.................... 15

Writing Workshop 3 – Expository Writing: Compare and Contrast.. 25

Writing Workshop 4 – Narrative Writing: Short Story 35

Writing Workshop 5 – Response to Expository Text.............. 49

Writing Workshop 6 – Research Writing 67

Writing Workshop 7 – Narrative Nonfiction..................... 79

Writing Workshop 8 – Poetry................................ 91

Writing Workshop 9 – Script Writing 101

Writing Workshop 10 – Procedural Texts: Business Letters 117

GRAMMAR HANDBOOK

Part 1: Grammar 127

Part 2: Usage.. 129

Part 3: Style.. 140

Part 4: Mechanics...................................... 142

GRAMMAR ACTIVITIES

UNIT 1

Parts of Speech Overview 151

Verbs Overview 153

Phrases 155

Incorporating Quoted Text..................................... 157

UNIT 2

Punctuating Pauses, Breaks, and Omissions 159

Active and Passive Voice 161

Mood.. 163

UNIT 3

Participles and Participial Phrases............................ 165

Clauses.. 167

Commas with Nonessential Elements 169

UNIT 4

Verbals and Verbal Phrases 171

Pronoun–Antecedent Agreement 173

Apostrophes 175

Introduction

SpringBoard instruction in writing is addressed in two integrated ways:
• through project-based, scaffolded writing assessments in the student texts
• through SpringBoard writing workshops

To support students in becoming effective writers, these writing workshops offer guided experiences in specific rhetorical and grammar and usage skills, emphasizing practice and mastery of specific writing modes. The SpringBoard writing workshops offer direct writing instruction to support and extend mastery of the writing process and commonly assessed written products. Each workshop guides students through the writing of three separate texts in the specific mode being taught: one that is constructed as a class with direct guidance from the teacher, one that is peer constructed with teacher support, and one that is written independently.

Instructional Design

The SpringBoard writing workshops follow an instructional sequence designed to support students in their initial writing efforts and to provide practice to help them gain independent writing skills. Each workshop is composed of four activities that are structured to provide a gradual release of control, moving students from a class writing exercise to writing independently.

Activity 1 requires students to read a mentor text and to study it from the perspective of a writer to understand structure and stylistic techniques the author uses to create meaning in the text.

Activity 2 has students participate in a class-constructed writing practice in which the teacher guides students in writing a model text that incorporates learning from the analysis of the mentor text in Activity 1. Activity 2 enables the most proficient writer in the room—the teacher—to model SpringBoard writing strategies and to help students move successfully through the writing process to create a text that adheres to the Learning Targets outlined for the activity.

Activity 3 has students work in collaborative groups to apply knowledge learned from the first two activities and to produce a writing product that meets the expectations for writing in the specific mode. For this activity, students do the planning and writing, while teachers monitor their work and provide mini-lessons as needed to differentiate instruction and to support student learning.

Activity 4 requires students to work on their own to produce writing that demonstrates all the characteristics of the mode they have been learning and practicing.

Vertical Articulation of Writing Skills and Concepts

The SpringBoard writing workshops provide extensive coverage in essential modes, as well as in creative modes. For each writing mode, there is a clear sequence of writing development, taking students through organizational structure, presentation of ideas, use of stylistic techniques, use of sentence structure for effect, and incorporation of grammar and language conventions. Each writing workshop is accompanied by a Scoring Guide that outlines the performance expectations for each writing mode and provides accountability for the learning targets identified at each grade level.

In the upper grades these writing workshops provide several opportunities for students to practice responding to writing prompts that are modeled on AP-type prompts, thus preparing them to demonstrate the skills needed for college entrance exams, AP assessments, and high-stakes state assessments.

Through writing experiences in the SpringBoard texts as well as in these writing workshops, students will be prepared to write in any tested genre and will gain the following:
- Reading-writing connections that result in transferable literacy skills
- Ability to produce writing in a variety of modes
- Experience in using research to inform writing and to support credible argument
- Skills in collaborating and communicating with other writers
- Language development in writing and speech, as well as embedded grammar instruction that focuses on structure and effect in writing

Development of Language Skills with Grammar Activities

The Grammar Activities included with the SpringBoard Writing Workshop complement the SpringBoard English Language Arts program and can be used to enhance language instruction throughout the year. For each grade, the Grammar Activities are organized into units corresponding to the SpringBoard English Language Arts units. The activities per grade can be assigned to students in conjunction with the Language & Writer's Craft and Grammar & Usage features in the English Language Arts Student Edition, or can be introduced more flexibly whenever students struggle with a specific grammar topic.

The topics covered by the Grammar Activities, such as pronoun usage, punctuation, and sentence structures, align to the California Common Core State Standards and will support students in their writing practice. Learning Targets for each lesson highlight the standards addressed in student-friendly language. Each activity features direct instruction on a language topic and opportunities for students to identify and correct common grammar and usage errors independently. The Teacher Edition provides information about when to use the activity in the ELA sequence, additional instructional content for teachers who would like to use the activity as a mini-lesson, and suggested student responses.

The Grammar Activities in conjunction with the Writing Workshops provide essential support for students to develop their language skills and grow as effective writers in the SpringBoard English Language Arts classroom.

The Writing Process: Strategies for Writing

Learning Targets

- Produce clear and coherent writing in which the development, organization, and style are appropriate to task, purpose, and audience.
- With some guidance and support from peers and adults, develop and strengthen writing as needed by planning, revising, editing, rewriting, or trying a new approach, focusing on how well purpose and audience have been addressed.
- Demonstrate command of the conventions of standard English grammar and usage when writing or speaking.
- Demonstrate command of the conventions of standard English capitalization, punctuation, and spelling when writing.
- Use knowledge of language and its conventions when writing, speaking, reading, or listening.
- Engage effectively in a range of collaborative discussions (one-on-one, in groups, and teacher-led) with diverse partners on middle school topics, texts, and issues, building on others' ideas and expressing your own clearly.

LEARNING STRATEGIES
Quickwrite, Previewing, Think-Pair-Share, Graphic Organizer, RAFT, Think Aloud, Generating Questions, Brainstorming, Self/ Peer Editing, Marking the Text, Sharing and Responding

The Writing Process

Writing is a recursive process, meaning that writers may repeat the steps of drafting, revising, and polishing many times before they are satisfied with their product. Successful writers are flexible in how they approach a writing situation. They use a variety of strategies to carry out and manage the task of composing. This workshop is designed to help you understand the stages of the writing process and the strategies that will help you develop your own writing process.

To complete this workshop you will work with your teacher and your classmates to follow the writing process in planning, drafting, organizing, and revising and editing a model piece of writing. You will then use the writing process to independently write a piece of your choosing.

ACTIVITY 1

Exploring the Writing Process

Before Reading

1. What do you know about the writing process? Describe the stages you go through, from beginning to end, to publish a piece of writing.

Stages of the Writing Process

2. Consider the traditional stages of the writing process represented below and placed in random order. Work with a partner to brainstorm the role of the writer within each stage of the writing process.

Writer's Role	
Sharing and Responding	Prewriting
Editing	Publishing
Revising	Drafting

Writing Process Graphic

3. After discussing the writing process, use your imagination to create a graphic representation of the writing process that shows its stages and their recursive nature.

During Reading

As you read the following student sample, read the text from the perspective of a writer.

4. As you read this text, identify as much as you can about the writer and his viewpoint. Highlight statements the writer makes that present his point of view.

Sample Text

My Long Distance Life

by Nick Sheff

I was born in Berkeley, where I lived in a small house in the hills surrounded by firs and redwoods. My mom, my dad and me. As early as I can remember, there was arguing. When I was 4, my parents decided that they could no longer live together.

That same year, my mom moved to Los Angeles, and a therapist was hired to decide where I would live. My dad called her my worry doctor. Playing with a dollhouse in her office, I showed her the mother's room on one side and the father's room on the other. When she asked me about the little boy's room, I told her he didn't know where he would sleep.

Though I was very young, I accepted my parents' separation and divorce and somehow knew it wasn't my fault. Yet I was intensely afraid. Not only was my mom more than 500 miles away, but she had a new husband. My dad had a new girlfriend, and my custody was unresolved. Everyone said I'd spend time with both parents, but I wanted to know where I would live.

The therapist finally decided I'd stay with my dad during the school year and visit my mom on long holidays and for the summers. I began flying between two cities and two different lives. I've probably earned enough miles for a round-trip ticket to Mars. Some people love to fly, but I dreaded the trips.

For the first year, one of my parents would accompany me on the flights. At 6, I started traveling on my own. I would pack my toys and clothes in a Hello Kitty backpack and say goodbye to my parent at the gate. The flight attendant would lead me onto the plane.

When I was 7, the woman sitting next to me on the plane tried to convert me to Christianity. A few years later I was on a flight with such bad turbulence that the luggage compartments opened and the man behind me threw up. When I was 12 and on my way to L.A. for Christmas, a lady refused to check her bag and shoved a flight attendant. We couldn't take off for two hours; the police came and dragged her off, to the cheering of other passengers. But flying was just part of what made long-distance joint custody so difficult.

I remember the last day of school in sixth grade. All my friends made plans to go to the beach together—all my friends, but not me. I couldn't join them because I had to fly to L.A. It wasn't that I didn't want to see my mom and stepdad. I just didn't want to leave my friends. As the school year came to a close, I began to shut down. I hated saying goodbye for the summer. It was easier to put up a wall, to pretend I didn't care. My dad drove to school with my packed bags. My friends went off together and I headed to the airport.

Arriving in L.A., I was excited to see my mom and stepdad. It had been almost three months since my last visit. But it took a while to adjust. Each set of parents had different rules, values and concerns.

My Notes

I am 16 now and I still travel back and forth, but it's mostly up to me to decide when. I've chosen to spend more time with my friends at the expense of visits with my mom. When I do go to L.A. it's like my stepdad put it: I have a cameo role in their lives. I say my lines and I'm off. It's painful.

What's the toll of this arrangement? I'm always missing somebody. When I'm in northern California, I miss my mom and stepdad. But when I'm in L.A., I miss hanging out with my friends, my other set of parents and little brother and sister. After all those back-and-forth flights, I've learned not to get too emotionally attached. I have to protect myself.

Many of my friends' parents are divorced. The ones whose mom and dad live near each other get to see both their parents more. These kids can go to school plays and dances on the weekend, and see their friends when they want. But others have custody arrangements like mine. One friend whose dad moved to New Hampshire sees him at Christmas and for one month during the summer. My girlfriend's dad lives in Alaska. They know what I know: it's not fair.

No child should be subjected to the hardship of long-distance joint custody. To prevent it, maybe there should be an addition to the marriage vows: Do you promise to have and to hold, for richer and for poorer, in sickness and in health, as long as you both shall live? And if you ever have children and wind up divorced, do you promise to stay within the same geographical area as your kids? Actually, since people often break those vows, maybe it should be a law: If you have children, you must stay near them. Or how about some common sense? If you move away from your children, you have to do the traveling to see them.

In two years I go to college. I'll be living away from both homes, which will present new problems, such as where I will spend holidays. Whatever happens, I'll continue to build my relationships with both my parents, my siblings and my friends.

Before I have children of my own, I'll use my experiences to help make good decisions about whom I choose to marry. However, if I do get a divorce, I will put my children's needs first. I will stay near them no matter what happens.

After Reading

5. When you have finished reading, respond to the questions below in the space provided. Be prepared to discuss your answers with your classmates.

   a. **Purpose:** What was the writer's purpose for composing this text? Was it to inform, to entertain, to persuade, to reflect, or to share an experience? Explain.

   b. **Audience:** Who is the intended audience for this piece?

   c. **Position/Thesis:** What central idea and/or message did the writer want to convey?

d. **Mode:** Identify the writing mode and essential features. Discuss how the mode is used to support the purpose of the writing, and describe the position of the writer.

ACADEMIC VOCABULARY
Mode describes the purposes for writing. The three most commonly used modes of writing are narrative, expository, and persuasive.
Transitions are words or phrases that help carry a thought from one sentence to another, from one idea to another, or from one paragraph to another so that there are no abrupt jumps or breaks between ideas.

e. **Organization:** How has the writer chosen to organize his writing?

f. **Transitions:** What words does the writer use to connect and clarify relationships between ideas and create and move the reader from one part of the essay to the next?

Check Your Understanding

With a partner, evaluate the effectiveness of blending the two modes of writing. How would the essay have been different if it had only been narrative, or only expository?

ACTIVITY 2
Working Through the Writing Process as a Class

Stage 1: Choosing a Topic

As a writer, you may have the opportunity to choose an original topic for your writing or you may write in response to a prompt. Either way, you will benefit from going through the stages of the writing process.

"It seems to me that writing is a marvelous way of making sense of one's life, both for the writer and the reader." —John Cheever

1. Use the chart below to brainstorm a list in each category of potential writing topics for you to explore and share with your readers.

Potential Writing Topics			
What are some of the best things that have happened to you?	What are some of the worst things that have happened to you?	What are some of the most significant learning experiences you have encountered?	What are some other ideas for topics of interest to you?

2. Share the lists with a partner. As you listen to one another and discover similar ideas, add them to your initial list of potential writing topics.

3. Read through your list, and circle one topic from each category that is of particular interest to you and that you can write about fully. Select one circled topic to share with a partner. Use the following questions to guide your partner discussion:
   • What happened?
   • Who was involved, and how did the people involved respond?
   • Why is this experience memorable?
   • Who might benefit from your sharing this experience?

4. Explore your **topic** further using the RAFT strategy to explore the writer's persona or **role** and purpose, to identify possible **audiences**, and to select an appropriate format or mode of writing to convey the purpose.

Introducing the Strategy: RAFT

Primarily used to generate text, the RAFT strategy helps writers plan for writing by focusing on the writer's role, audience, format, and topic. RAFT can also be used to analyze a text by examining and identifying the role of the speaker, the intended audience, the format, and the topic of the text.

Role of the writer: What perspective or persona will you take on to meet your goals for writing and to establish a connection with your readers?	Audience: Who is your target audience? What information might you include to capture their interest?	Topic: What is your purpose for writing this piece? Use strong verbs to describe your purpose.	Format: What writing mode or genre would be best to represent this topic? Explain.

5. Now use this sentence frame to consider your goal for writing.

From the perspective of a(an) _____ I am writing a(an) _____
                                        Role   Format

to _____ my _____ that _____, ___
   Topic   Audience   Topic   _____.

Stage 2: Prewriting

"I suppose some writers begin with a phrase, an idea, or a concept. I always begin with an image." —Gabriel García Márquez

1. How do you begin to explore a subject before writing? Consider what you currently know and need to know in order to guide the exploration of your selected topic.

2. Review the purpose of the prewriting strategies (e.g., free-writing and looping, mapping, outlining, sketching, or webbing) in the *Resources* section of your SpringBoard book. Select an appropriate strategy, and begin prewriting to generate ideas, explore connections among them, and organize information.

Introducing the Strategy: Free-Writing, Looping, and Adding

Free-writing consists of using a fluid brainstorming process to write without constraints in order to generate content and clarify and convey the writer's purpose.

After free-writing, **looping** focuses on one section of a text which is identified to promote elaboration or the generation of new ideas for that section. This process is repeated to further develop ideas from the newly generated segments.

Adding consists of making conscious choices to enhance a text by adding additional words, phrases, sentences, or ideas.

Sample Looping and Adding to part of a free writing activity:
"Arriving in L.A., I was excited to see my mom and stepdad. It had been almost three months since my last visit. But it took a while to adjust. Each set of parents had different rules, values, and concerns."

Material added as a result of looping: "But it took a while to adjust." With my father, I am an only child, and I have an active social life, but with my mom and step-dad, my time is spent entirely with my younger brothers.

3. Review your prewriting, and consider how the ideas generated fit your goals and purpose for writing. This might be an appropriate time to settle upon a preliminary position or controlling idea to shape your point of view or your underlying message.

4. Think about the format or mode you selected while completing the RAFT organizer, and consider the conventions of the format in preparation for a first draft. Consult resources as necessary to familiarize yourself with the organizational structure of your selected type of text.

Check Your Understanding

You have completed the Prewriting stages in the writing process. Explain why these stages are important steps before the actual drafting of your writing. How can they help make drafting your writing easier and more fully developed?

Stage 3: Drafting the Text

Once you have finished the prewriting stage, you are ready to create a working draft of your text. Using your **RAFT** thinking, your **free-writing, looping, adding** and any other brainstorming, you are ready to write.

"Writing should be like riding a bike down a hill, bouncing along, going fast."
—*Don Murray*

1. Revisit the Writer's Role graphic organizer and discuss how this quote pertains to the drafting stage of the writing process. Then describe your experiences with drafting in the past.

2. Before you begin drafting, think about organizing your ideas. Create a preliminary organizational structure by creating a topic outline that shows what ideas you will include and in what order the ideas will be developed. Be sure to focus your attention on building ideas to create a focused and coherent piece of writing. For help in doing this, examine and track the organization of the model essay. Note how the narrative develops and when it shifts to explaining or expository development.

3. Once you have completed your draft, read through it and use looping to pinpoint areas where you might further refine your writing for clarity and detail in preparation for sharing your draft with your peers. Consider the areas of the draft where you would like peer support, and note appropriate questions and/or comments to share in a small group.

Stage 4: Sharing and Responding in Writing Groups

"Reader response drives revision." —Kelly Gallagher

1. Revisit the Writer's Role graphic organizer, and discuss how this quote pertains to the sharing and responding stage of the writing process.

2. In a writing group, all members work collaboratively to assist the writer through the revision process by asking clarifying questions that may help to develop a quality piece of writing. Look at the "Roles of the Participants in Writing Groups" for things to consider while sharing and responding.

Roles of the Participants in Writing Groups

Job	Guidelines	Response Prompts
The reader: **Reads the text silently, then aloud. Begins the conversation after reading.**	The reader's focus is to share an understanding of the writer's words. The reader will also see the physical structure of the draft and may comment on that. The reader follows all listeners' guidelines.	Reader's and listeners' compliments: • I liked…about this piece • This piece made me feel…. • This piece reminded me of….
The listener: **Takes notes and prepares open-ended questions for the writer or makes constructive statements.**	The listeners begin with positive statements. The listeners use "I" statements and talk about the writing, not the writer. The listeners make a statement but must support it with a reason.	Listeners' comments and suggestions: • I really enjoyed the part where…. • What parts are you having trouble with? • What do you plan to do next? • I was confused when….
The writer: **Listens to the draft, takes notes, responds to questions, and asks the writing group questions.**	As his or her work is being read aloud by another, the writer can get an overall impression of the piece. Also, the writer can take notes on what might need to be changed. The writer asks the writing group questions to get feedback that will lead to effective revision.	Writer's comments/questions: • My initial writing goals were…. I'm struggling with or I'm requesting support with…. • What do you want to know more about? • What part does not make sense and/or align with the goals I stated? • What section of the text does not work?

3. Use the Roles of Participants in Writing Groups to guide your writing group as you share your writing with each other and provide feedback for one another to help lead to focused revision.

Stage 5: Revision

"Rewriting is when playwriting really gets to be fun. In baseball, you only get three swings and you're out. In rewriting, you get almost as many swings as you want and you know, sooner or later, you'll hit the ball." —Neil Simon

1. Describe your experience with revision. What revision strategies have you used in the past and what effect did they have on your text?

2. In your writing groups, you received feedback on what is working well in your draft and suggestions for improvement. Review your notes, read through your draft, evaluate it for clarity of focus, progression of ideas, organization and development of ideas. Consider which writing group suggestions are appropriate to improve the draft.

3. Review the revision strategies and choose one or more to use as you revise your draft, considering the priorities listed below, your own insights, and the feedback from your writing group.

Revision Checklist

Revision Priorities	Strategy	Consult Resources
Write an engaging lead to hook readers.		
Sequence ideas to create coherence in my text.		
Develop ideas fully with examples and details as evidence		
Create a conclusion that follows from the ideas presented		

4. Complete your revision checklist and create a plan to begin revising your draft. You might want to use a computer to type your next draft. Print multiple copies to share in your next writing group meeting.

Stage 6: Editing

"The writer will also discover surprises in the process of editing, and the writer should delight in them." –Donald Murray

1. Reread your notes on editing from "Writer's Role" descriptions. Describe your experiences with editing and the editing strategies or techniques you have used in the past.

2. Use grammar reference sources to identify the following punctuation marks and describe their function.

Mark	Name	Purpose/Function
!	Exclamation point	End mark used to indicate a command or excited remark
.	Period	End mark that ends a declarative sentence
?	Question mark	End mark that indicates a question
,	Comma	Mark that indicates a pause
;	Semicolon	Mark that indicates a pause between two complete thoughts
:	Colon	Mark that precedes a list
--	Dash	Mark that indicates more text is to follow
( )	Parentheses	Marks that surround text that is not essential to the sentence
" "	Quotation marks	Mark that surrounds direct quotations
/	Slash or diagonal	Mark that indicates a line break in poetry

3. Think about how you might use a punctuation mark to express who you are. Then complete the sentence frame below:

I identify myself as a _____ because_____.
                               (punctuation mark)

4. Use the *Common Proofreading Marks* to self-edit your current draft. Share your edited draft in your next writing group meeting.

Common Proofreading Marks

Proofreading Symbol	Explanation	Example
⌃	Insert a comma.	My cat has one white paw two brown paws, and one brown and white paw.
⌄	Insert an apostrophe or a single quotation mark.	Her mothers job involves a lot of travel.
⌄⌄	Insert double quotation marks.	Have you read the poem, My Father's Son?
⊙	Add a period.	The roses are in bloom
¶	Begin a new paragraph.	"Where will you be at 5?" I asked. "On the bus home," she replied.

5. Review the grammar topics on the *Editor's/Writer's Checklist* graphic organizer and highlight the concepts in the first column that are unfamiliar to you. Take notes on grammar rules and copy sample sentences from published writers into the graphic organizer to refer to when you edit your next draft.

Editor's/Writer's Checklist

Topics	Editing Rule	Example
Capitalization: Did you capitalize the first word of sentences, proper nouns, and titles?		
Complete Sentences: Are all of your sentences complete thoughts? Correct all fragments and run-ons that might be present in your draft.		
Consistent Voice: Is your point of view consistent? (first, second, or third person)?		
Subject-Verb Agreement: Are verb endings correct? Do all of your subjects agree with verbs in person and number?		
Pronouns: Is pronoun use appropriate and consistent?		
Varied Sentences: Are your sentences (simple, compound, complex) and lengths varied for interest and emphasis?		
Spell Check: Circle words that might be misspelled. Use available resources (e.g., spell check, dictionary, or peer) to correct errors in spelling.		
Typographical Errors: Read your draft aloud, and carefully watch for typographical errors. Correct errors.		

Stage 7: Publishing

"The best way out is always through." —Robert Frost

1. Describe your experiences with publishing your writing for a larger audience.

2. After completing a written piece, a writer has many choices for publication. Brainstorm a list of publishing options available to you.

3. In preparation for completing a final draft, consider the following:
   - If appropriate, review your research on the conventions of your selected genre. Type your final draft and adhere to appropriate formatting. Incorporate illustrations into your final if they support your writing and add reader interest.
   - Brainstorm a list of possible titles by listing key words or phrases. Identify a word or phrase that captures the central idea of your text. Choose an appropriate title for your final draft.

4. Your teacher will provide you with the final guidelines for publication. Take notes on those guidelines, and revise your draft accordingly.

Check Your Understanding

Now that you have gone through the stages of the writing process as a group, consider what you have learned about yourself as a writer. Describe your writing process, which might be unique to you, and your growth as a writer. Revisit the writing process graphic you created in Activity 1, and consider whether it is still accurate. Modify it as needed in order to capture your process for writing, and create or select a quote to accompany your visual. In your writing group, share your visual.

a. Discuss your writing process.
b. Explain how you have developed as a writer.

Working Through the Writing Process Independently

WRITING PROMPT: Use your understanding of your writing process to develop an original text. Choose a topic, a genre, and an audience to which your topic will appeal. The following is an overview of the writing process presented in Activity 2. Use it as a reference as you craft your next piece.

➢ **Prewriting**
- Review your *Potential Writing Topics* list and select another topic of interest for you to take through the writing process.
- Use the RAFT strategy to establish a preliminary target audience, topic, position, and genre.
- Choose an appropriate prewriting strategy to generate content and consider a preliminary organizational structure.

➢ **Drafting**
- Review ideas and information generated from prewriting to create a draft.
- Read through your draft to refine it for clarity and coherence in preparation for sharing it with your peers.

➢ **Sharing and Responding**
- Work collaboratively within writing groups to provide effective responses that will lead to revision.
- Share your draft multiple times for help with revising and editing.

➢ **Revising**
- Review and evaluate your draft to make any appropriate changes.
- Consider the feedback received from peers or your teacher, and decide how you will incorporate those suggestions into your next draft.
- Create a "Revision Checklist" that identifies what needs to be done with the draft as well as the strategies and resources needed to accomplish the task.

➢ **Editing**
- Review your draft and edit it for conventions of standard written English and usage (e.g., grammar and conventions) appropriate for the genre.
- Consult additional resources (e.g., mentor texts, handbooks, style manuals, dictionaries, spell check, thesaurus, and peer editors) to correct errors in spelling, capitalization, grammar, and punctuation.
- Read through your draft and self-edit it using proofreading marks to signal changes that need to be made in the final draft.

> **Publishing**
> - Consider multiple venues to publish your work.
> - Produce a final draft that follows guidelines specified by your teacher, which might require, for instance, a typed or legible handwritten draft, an original title, and formatting appropriate for the genre selected.

When you finish this writing project, complete a written self-evaluation of your process and your finished piece. Attach your evaluation to your writing project.
- What do you think you did particularly well in this piece of writing?
- Locate the best sentence in your draft, and explain why this line is so powerful.
- If you could spend more time, what would you do to make the draft better?
- What have you learned about writing and about yourself as a writer?

SCORING GUIDE

Scoring Criteria	Exemplary	Proficient	Emerging	Incomplete
Ideas	The essay • asserts an original focus on an idea or concept to be developed • develops specific ideas skillfully and fully using examples, details and/or evidence	The essay • presents a clear focus on an idea or concept for development • develops ideas clearly using examples, details and/or evidence	The essay • presents a limited and/or unfocused concept or central idea • presents ideas vague or incomplete with examples, details and/or evidence	The essay • lacks a clear claim or focus • ideas are not developed nor supported with relevant or clarifying examples, details and/or evidence
Structure	The essay • leads with a convincing and engaging introduction • uses meaningful transitional devices to guide understanding of the relationship among ideas • logically organizes and effectively sequences ideas • provides a thoughtful conclusion that extends thinking	The essay • presents a clear and focused introduction • uses transitions to create coherence • orders evidence in a way that supports understanding • provides a conclusion that connects the larger ideas presented	The essay • contains an underdeveloped and/or unfocused introduction • makes limited use of transitional devices • does not present ideas in a logical order • contains an underdeveloped or unfocused conclusion	The essay • contains a minimal or incomplete introduction • uses few or no meaningful transitions • uses a confusing organization • provides minimal concluding material or none at all
Use of Language	The essay • uses a variety of sentence structures to enhance the effect • uses diction that is deliberately chosen for the topic, audience, and purpose • incorporates rhetorical devices skillfully to advance ideas presented • demonstrates technical command of conventions of standard English	The essay • uses a variety of sentence structures • uses diction that is appropriate to the topic, audience, and purpose • incorporates rhetorical devices effectively • demonstrates general command of standard English conventions; minor errors do not interfere with meaning	The essay • shows little or no variety in sentence structure • uses inappropriate diction for the topic, audience, and purpose • uses few or no rhetorical devices in the text • demonstrates limited command of standard English conventions; errors interfere with meaning	The essay • shows no variety in sentence structure • uses little or no purposeful diction • uses no rhetorical devices effectively • demonstrates poor command of standard English conventions; multiple serious errors interfere with meaning

Argumentative Writing

Learning Targets
- Write arguments to support claims with clear reasons and relevant evidence.
- Produce clear and coherent writing in which the development, organization, and style are appropriate to task, purpose, and audience.
- With some guidance and support from peers and adults, develop and strengthen writing as needed by planning, revising, editing, rewriting, or trying a new approach, focusing on how well purpose and audience have been addressed.
- Demonstrate command of the conventions of standard English grammar and usage when writing or speaking.
- Demonstrate command of the conventions of standard English capitalization, punctuation, and spelling when writing.
- Use knowledge of language and its conventions when writing, speaking, reading or listening.
- Engage effectively in a range of collaborative discussions (one-on-one, in groups, and teacher-led)with diverse partners on grade 8 topics, texts, and issues, building on others' ideas and expressing their own clearly.

LEARNING STRATEGIES
Activating Prior Knowledge, Brainstorming, Think-Pair-Share, Discussion Groups, Close Reading, Sharing and Responding, Marking the Text, Graphic Organizer, Outlining, Drafting, Adding, Deleting, Rearranging, Substituting, Revising Prior Work, Self-Editing, Peer-Editing

Writing an Argumentative Essay

Argumentative technique is an important skill writers use to influence the attitudes or actions of their intended audience regarding a wide variety of issues. Effective argumentation involves clearly identifying issues, anticipating and responding to objections, presenting support for a position, and using clear and relevant reasoning to help convince an audience.

As you learn about argumentative writing, you will work with your teacher and with your classmates to construct two argumentative essays. You will then use these models for your own independent writing.

ACTIVITY 1
Discovering the Elements of an Argumentative Essay

Before Reading
1. Review the difference between a claim and a counterclaim. Why will a good, strong claim always carry within it a justifiable counterclaim? Explain how relevant and sufficient evidence is important for convincing the reader to believe a writer's claim.

During Reading
2. As you read this text, identify the writer's viewpoint and highlight the claim being made. Underline the evidence that supports that claim. Circle anything that suggests claims that are opposed to the writer's claims.

About the Author: William Lyon Phelps (1865–1943) was an American educator, literary critic, and author. He served as a professor of English at Yale University from 1901 to 1933. His works include *Advance of the English Novel* and *Essays on Modern Dramatists*. On April 6, 1933, he delivered this speech during a radio broadcast.

His reverence for books was not shared by everyone, especially those in Nazi Germany. On May 10, 1933, the Nazis staged an event unseen since the Middle Ages in which young German students from universities formerly regarded as among the finest in the world gathered in Berlin and other German cities to burn books with "un-German" ideas.

The Pleasure of Books

The habit of reading is one of the greatest resources of mankind; and we enjoy reading books that belong to us much more than if they are borrowed. A borrowed book is like a guest in the house; it must be treated with punctiliousness, with a certain considerate formality. You must see that it sustains no damage; it must not suffer while under your roof. You cannot leave it carelessly, you cannot mark it, you cannot turn down the pages, you cannot use it familiarly. And then, some day, although this is seldom done, you really ought to return it.

But your own books belong to you; you treat them with that affectionate intimacy that annihilates formality. Books are for use, not for show; you should own no book that you are afraid to mark up, or afraid to place on the table, wide open and face down. A good reason for marking favorite passages in books is that this practice enables you to remember more easily the significant sayings, to refer to them quickly, and then in later years, it is like visiting a forest where you once blazed a trail. You have the pleasure of going over the old ground, and recalling both the intellectual scenery and your own earlier self.

Everyone should begin collecting a private library in youth; the instinct of private property, which is fundamental in human beings, can here be cultivated with every advantage and no evils. One should have one's own bookshelves, which should not have doors, glass windows, or keys; they should be free and accessible to the hand as well as to the eye. The best of mural decorations is books; they are more varied in color and appearance than any wallpaper, they are more attractive in design, and they have the prime advantage of being separate personalities, so that if you sit alone in the room in the firelight, you are surrounded with intimate friends. The knowledge that they are there in plain view is both stimulating and refreshing. You do not have to read them all. Most of my indoor life is spent in a room containing six thousand books; and I have a stock answer to the invariable question that comes from strangers. "Have you read all of these books?"

"Some of them twice." This reply is both true and unexpected.

There are of course no friends like living, breathing, corporeal men and women; my devotion to reading has never made me a recluse. How could it? Books are of the people, by the people, for the people. Literature is the immortal part of history; it is the best and most enduring part of personality. But book-friends have this advantage over living friends; you can enjoy the most truly aristocratic society in the world whenever you want it. The great dead are beyond our physical reach, and the great living are usually almost as inaccessible; as for our personal friends and acquaintances, we cannot always see them. Perchance they are asleep, or away on a journey. But in a private library, you can at any moment converse with Socrates or Shakespeare or Carlyle or Dumas or Dickens or Shaw or Barrie or Galsworthy. And there is no doubt that in these books you see these men at their best. They wrote for you. They "laid themselves out," they did their ultimate best to entertain you, to make a favorable impression. You are necessary to them as an audience is to an actor; only instead of seeing them masked, you look into their innermost heart of heart.

After Reading

3. When you have finished reading, respond to the questions below in the space provided. Be prepared to discuss your answers with your classmates.

   a. **Purpose:** What is the writer's purpose for writing this argument? (Refer to the sentence in the first paragraph that you highlighted for the claim or thesis of the essay.)

   b. **Audience:** Who do you think the writer had in mind as an audience for this argument? To whom do the reasons and evidence seem addressed? How do you know?

   c. **Support:** What facts, examples, and personal experiences does the writer present as evidence to support the argument? What evidence is most relevant and effective, and why?

   d. **Opposing Claims or Viewpoints:** What opposing viewpoints does the writer acknowledge?

e. **Organization:** How does the thesis statement set up the logical organization of the essay?

f. **Transitions:** What words does the writer use to connect and clarify relationships between ideas and create and move the reader from one part of the essay to the next?

g. **Sources:** What sources does the writer cite? How do those sources support the writer's claim with relevant evidence? Do the sources appear credible?

Check Your Understanding
To what degree does this speech by Phelps include all the elements of a well-constructed argument?

ACTIVITY 2
Writing an Argumentative Class Essay

WRITING PROMPT: With your class, create an essay that argues for the collection of something that may not normally be considered collectible or interesting or feasible, such as pennies, video games, sports shoes, or LPs, etc.

Be sure your topic and argument meet the requirements listed in the learning targets for argumentative texts.
- Establish a claim consisting of a clear thesis or position.
- Use formal language that is appropriate for your purpose and audience.
- Include relevant and clear evidence that supports the claim.
- Include a variety of credible evidence based on fact and experience rather than opinion.
- Identify and address potential audience concerns and/or questions.
- Uses both indicative and imperative moods in grammar.

Refer to the Scoring Guide for this writing task to help you understand where to focus your attention and efforts.

ACADEMIC VOCABULARY

Evidence is said to be relevant if it is closely related to the issue or topic.

A credible source is one that is convincing or believable because it is reliable, accurate, and trustworthy.

Prewriting

1. Read and mark the writing prompt above to clarify the task.

2. As a class, brainstorm ideas for the class-generated essay and create a list of possible topics about which people might have alternative viewpoints.

3. With your class, choose a topic for the essay and write that topic here.

4. Consider, anticipate, and respond to possible audience opposing viewpoints. What are some of the views or attitudes that might prevent your idea from being adopted? How will you address this resistance?

5. To present a convincing argument, a writer must have an opinion about a topic upon which to build a claim. The claim presents the writer's position, or thesis. One way to state a claim is to present the claim and an opposing viewpoint in the same sentence. For example:

   SAMPLE: Though money is meant to be spent, collecting coins is educational and can turn into a financial windfall.

   Use the sentence pattern above to write the claim for the sample argumentative essay.

   While it is true that

6. In your writing groups, practice using this sentence pattern to create a thesis statement that presents your topic, claim, and a counterclaim.

7. Next, the class must decide the order in which to present your claim, counterclaim, and evidence you will provide to support your opinions. Working with your teacher, generate a class-constructed topic outline of the overall organizational plan for your argumentative writing.

Drafting

8. Working with your teacher and classmates, draft the introduction to your argumentative essay. Be sure to include the following elements:
   - Lead, or hook (the attention grabber)
   - Context (the situation that establishes the topic and its importance)
   - Thesis (the position of the class on the topic), using a complex sentence as in the model

9. You have learned how to develop paragraphs that form the body of your essay using
   - **Topic sentence**—a reason in support of your claim
   - **Evidence**—facts, stories, experiences, etc., that support your reasoning
   - **Commentary**—an explanation of the significance of the evidence or its connection to the topic sentence
   - **Transitions**—words or phrases that make the relationship between ideas obvious for the reader

   With your class, use these elements as you draft the body paragraphs for your class essay.

10. Working with your teacher, draft the conclusion to your argument. In this last paragraph, be sure to provide a call to action (encouragement to the audience to take action based on your claim). The conclusion should follow from and support your argument without introducing any ideas that have not already been addressed.

Check Your Understanding

Now that the class essay has been drafted, read the completed draft.
- Underline the topic and the claim or thesis in the introduction.
- Identify the reasons in each paragraph that support the claim.

Consider the following:
- What concerns and opposing viewpoints of the audience are addressed?
- Is there a strong connection (relevance) between the evidence and the claim in each body paragraph?
- Are the body paragraphs placed in a logical order that clearly supports the claim?
- How does the conclusion include a call to action and offer closure?
- What transitions connect the ideas being developed?

Now, refer to the Scoring Guide to help determine how well the essay meets the expectations.

Revising the Draft

Once you have examined and evaluated your drafted essay and used the Check Your Understanding questions, it is time to consider elements you may want to revise.

Revising for Language and Writer's Craft

Correct and varied use of verbs characterizes sophisticated writing. Verbs are the powerhouses of sentences and help create the mood and the tone in any mode, whether narrative, expository, or argumentative writing. A related form, the verbal, is another important grammatical element.

Grammatical mood of verbs: In grammar, mood does not describe an emotional state. Instead, **mood** is a form of the verb that conveys the writer's attitude toward a subject.

- The **indicative** mood is used to make factual statements or pose questions.
  "A borrowed book is like a guest in the house…"
  "Literature is the immortal part of history…"

- The **imperative** mood is used to express a request or command.
  "*Ask not* what your country can do for you."
  "*Ask* what you can do for your country."

- The **subjunctive** mood is used to show a wish, doubt, or anything contrary to fact.
  If I *were* to write in a book, I would be sure to own it.
  If I *were* asked to choose between books and friends, I would choose books.

- The **interrogative** mood indicates a state of questioning.
  "Have you read all of these books?"
  "How could it?"

The various moods, which convey different tones and attitudes, can be used for **rhetorical effect.**

Verbals: A verbal is a word formed from a verb but functioning as a different part of speech. One specific type of verbal is a gerund, a verb ending in *–ing* that acts as a noun. Gerunds and gerund phrases are used as nouns, and they can add liveliness to your writing.

Underline the gerunds and gerund phrases.

There's no crying in baseball!

Sleeping is an important aspect of maintaining mental health.

He is guilty of speaking too much and listening too little.

Notice how the *-ing* form of the verb is used differently in each of the following sentences: Which sentence includes a gerund?

John is standing in the middle of the road.

Standing in the middle of the road is dangerous.

Standing in the middle of the road, John flagged down a taxi cab.

Editing

11. Once you understand how to use verbs and verb moods for rhetorical effect, review your class-constructed essay. Use what you have learned to improve your writing. Then, as a final step, polish the final draft of the essay by editing for mistakes in spelling and conventions. Consider all the elements listed in the Use of Language section of the Scoring Guide. Be sure to make all corrections on your individual copy of the essay.

ACTIVITY 3
....
Writing an Argumentative Essay with Peers

WRITING PROMPT: Write an essay that argues for an activity that normally may not be considered feasible or popular, such as playing lacrosse, rock climbing, or ballroom dancing. Your job is to convince your audience of the activity's value.

Be sure your topic and argument meet the same learning targets listed for your class-constructed argumentative essay.

1. With your writing group, carefully review and apply the writing steps from the class-constructed argumentative essay:
   a. Brainstorm and choose a topic.
   b. Create a claim and thesis using a complex sentence pattern.
   c. Generate reasons and examples to support your claim.
   d. Anticipate alternate viewpoints and any opposing or alternate claims.
   e. Be sure your claim can be supported by logic and reasoning, not just personal preference.
   f. To plan your essay, generate a topic outline.
   g. Draft an introduction, body paragraphs, and conclusion.
   h. Plan for sharing and responding in preparation for revision.

Peer Review

2. You will evaluate and provide feedback for another group's essay, based on criteria established in the writing prompt and the Scoring Guide. Another group will review the work your group has done. Use the following revision checklist to guide your peer review.

Argumentative Essay Revision Checklist	
Issue/Topic	• Is the topic made clear in the introduction? Does it have importance or urgency?
Thesis (includes claim)	• Does the thesis combine the topic and a claim? • Does the writer give reasons for taking this position?
Support	• What facts, statistics, examples, and personal experiences does the writer use to support the thesis? • Does the writer use sound reasoning and relevant details? • Is the evidence accurate, current, and relevant to the topic?
Audience	• Who is the target audience? • Are the thesis, topic, and supporting ideas appropriate for the target audience?
Opposing Claims	• Does the writer identify opposing viewpoints clearly and fairly? • Doe the writer acknowledge and address opposing viewpoints with logic and relevant evidence?
Conclusion	• Does the writer conclude the essay in a way that convinces the audience to support the position and take action?

Revising/Editing

3. After rereading your group's draft, use the following strategies for revision:

   Adding: Are there changes you could make to strengthen the argument? Does anything need to be reorganized or explained more clearly?

   Rearranging: What revisions should be made to the structure of paragraphs or sentences?

   Deleting: Are there redundancies that should be eliminated? Is there information that does not directly support the central argument?

   Editing: Are there mistakes in conventions that should be corrected before the draft can be considered polished?

4. As you revise, also consider the use of grammatical mood and verbals in your draft. When appropriate, vary mood to create a rhetorical effect in the argument.

Independent Writing

WRITING PROMPT: With your class, create an essay that argues for collecting something that may not normally be considered collectible or interesting, such as pennies, video games, sports shoes, DVDs, LPs, or videos, etc. (Choose something other than the topic chosen for Activity 2.)

Be sure your topic and argument meet the requirements listed in the learning targets for argumentative texts.
• Establish a claim consisting of a clear thesis or position.
• Use formal language that is appropriate for your purpose and audience
• Include relevant and clear evidence that supports the claim.
• Include a variety of evidence based on fact and experience rather than opinion.
• Identify and address potential audience concerns and/or questions.
• Uses both indicative and imperative moods in grammar.

Use the process from your previous activities to accomplish your task.

SCORING GUIDE

Scoring Criteria	Exemplary	Proficient	Emerging	Incomplete
Ideas	The essay • establishes a strong, clear claim or position for an appropriate audience • supports claim with clear reasons and relevant evidence and effective commentary • anticipates and thoroughly addresses alternate viewpoints	The essay • presents a clear claim • supports with logical reasoning with relevant evidence and clear commentary • anticipates possible audience concerns	The essay • presents a limited or unfocused thesis or position • contains insufficient reasoning with evidence that sometimes confuses • does not anticipate potential alternate viewpoints	The essay • lacks a clear claim to be proven • contains irrelevant or insufficient reasoning • does not present or address counterclaims
Structure	The essay • leads with an effective and engaging introduction • effectively sequences ideas and uses meaningful transitions to clarify relationships among ideas • provides an insightful conclusion that follows from and supports the position	The essay • presents a clear and focused introduction • sequences ideas, and uses transitions to clarify relationships • provides a conclusion that connects the larger ideas presented in the essay.	The essay • contains an underdeveloped and/or unfocused introduction • presents disconnected ideas and limited use of transitions • contains an underdeveloped or unfocused conclusion.	The essay • contains a minimal or incomplete introduction • uses few or no meaningful transitions • uses a confusing organization for evidence and ideas • provides a minimal conclusion or none at all
Use of Language	The essay • uses a variety of sentence structures to enhance the persuasive effect • uses diction deliberately chosen for the topic, audience, and purpose • effectively and purposefully uses grammatical mood and verbals • demonstrates technical command of conventions of standard English	The essay • uses a variety of sentence structures • uses diction appropriate to the topic, audience, and purpose • employs grammatical mood and verbals • demonstrates general command of conventions; with only minor errors in grammar, punctuation, capitalization, or spelling	The essay • shows limited variety of sentence structure • uses inappropriate diction for the topic, audience, and purpose • uses irrelevant or inappropriate grammatical mood or verbals • contains errors in grammar, punctuation, capitalization, or spelling that interfere with meaning	The essay • shows little or no variety in sentence structure • uses inappropriate diction for the topic, audience, and purpose • does not use grammatical mood or verbals correctly • contains major errors in conventions that interfere with meaning

Expository Writing: Compare and Contrast

Learning Targets
- Write informative/explanatory texts to examine a topic and convey ideas, concepts, and information through the selection, organization, and analysis of relevant content.
- Produce clear and coherent writing in which the development, organization, and style are appropriate to task, purpose, and audience.
- With some guidance and support from peers and adults, develop and strengthen writing as needed by planning, revising, editing, rewriting, or trying a new approach, focusing on how well purpose and audience have been addressed.
- Demonstrate command of the conventions of standard English grammar and usage when writing or speaking.
- Demonstrate command of the conventions of standard English capitalization, punctuation, and spelling when writing.
- Use knowledge of language and its conventions when writing, speaking, reading, or listening.
- Engage effectively in a range of collaborative discussions (one-on-one, in groups, and teacher-led) with diverse partners on grade 8 topics, texts, and issues, building on others' ideas and expressing their own clearly.

LEARNING STRATEGIES
Brainstorming, Think-Pair-Share, Discussion Groups, Sharing and Responding, Marking the Text, Graphic Organizer, Outlining, Drafting, Adding, Deleting, Rearranging, Substituting, Revising Prior Work, Self-Editing/Peer-Editing

Writing an Expository Essay

The purpose of an expository essay is to communicate ideas and information to specific audiences for specific purposes. Expository essays are often written to define or describe a subject, to provide directions for how to do something, or to compare subjects by exploring how they are similar and different.

To complete this workshop on effective expository writing, you will work with your teacher and your classmates to construct two model compare-and-contrast expository essays. You will then use these models to write your own compare-and-contrast expository essay.

ACTIVITY 1
Discovering the Elements of a Compare and Contrast Essay

Before Reading
1. Define the terms *compare* and *contrast*.

2. The goal of a compare-and-contrast expository essay is to explore the similarities and differences between two subjects. What are some topics that would be interesting or useful to compare and contrast, and why? List several below.

During Reading

3. The following expository essay compares and contrasts characters from two short stories. Read the essay in order to identify the writer's **purpose** or main idea and make inferences about the writer's intended **audience**.

4. As you read, evaluate the writer's use of **evidence** to develop the topic. Evidence includes relevant facts, definitions, concrete details, quotations, or other information and examples. Underline or highlight the most relevant or effective examples.

My Notes

Sample Text

Like Hearts from Different Places

What could a teenage boy living in the mountains of Switzerland have in common with a boy growing up in tropical Trinidad? Rudi in James Ramsey Ullman's "A Boy and a Man" and Santo in Sam Selvon's "The Mouth Organ" do come from very different places and have different interests and abilities. However, they both are faithful to their dreams.

The contrasts between the two characters are obvious. Rudi is a rugged boy from the mountains of Switzerland. He shows courage and resourcefulness when he rescues Captain Winter from the crevasse into which he has fallen. This rescue is not completely surprising because Rudi has been brought up in a tradition of mountaineering. His father, killed in a climbing accident, was one of the greatest mountain guides in Switzerland. Unlike Rudi, Santo comes from a Caribbean island and has never seen snow. Also, in contrast with Rudi, Santo seems uninterested in athletics. He helps his father work in the fields, but he does not seem to be especially fond of exercise.

On a deeper level, however, the two boys are very similar. Rudi's most important traits are his curiosity about mountaineering and his faithfulness to his dream of climbing the Citadel. Although his mother and uncle try to keep him from climbing, he disobeys their rules and still hopes to conquer the mountain on which his father died. Like Rudi, Santo is alert and curious. When he hears about Father Christmas, he wants to know more. He learns more and begins to dream about receiving a gift from this magical man. Just as Rudi resists his family's commands, Santo holds on to his dream and ignores the discouraging words of his sister and mother.

Despite obvious differences, both boys share an important quality—faith. Rudi believes he can climb a mountain that has never been conquered. In the same way, Santo believes that Father Christmas will bring him a gift. This underlying similarity of two very different boys shows that we are all more alike than we know.

After Reading

5. When you have finished reading, respond to the following questions in the space provided. Be prepared to discuss your answers with your classmates.

   a. **Purpose:** What is the writer's purpose for writing this essay? (Refer to the first paragraph in which the writer introduces the topic.)

   b. **Audience:** Whom do you think the writer had in mind as an audience for this essay? How do you know?

   c. **Organization:** What is the purpose or main idea of each paragraph?

   d. **Evidence:** What examples and details does the writer use to support and develop the topic? What evidence is most relevant?

   e. **Transitions:** What words does the writer use to connect and clarify relationships among ideas and guide the reader from one part of the essay to the next?

   f. **Language and Style:** What are examples of precise and vivid diction (word choice) that the writer uses to explain and describe the topic?

Check Your Understanding

6. How did the sample text move from one topic (Rudi) to another (Santo) in order to convey the ideas clearly? Identify some of the methods used.

7. There are a number of decisions that could benefit from using the skills of comparing and contrasting, such as choosing a political candidate, deciding where to go on vacation, and deciding what classes to take. Think of three other decisions you might need to make that could benefit from comparing and contrasting the two options.

ACTIVITY 2

Writing an Expository Class Essay

WRITING PROMPT: Think about what you and your classmates eat for lunch. Write a multi-paragraph essay that compares and contrasts two different lunchtime meals (for example, salad versus pizza or school lunch versus home lunch). Be sure the essay
- Presents effective introductory and concluding paragraphs
- Contains a clearly stated purpose or controlling idea
- Is logically organized with appropriate facts and details
- Includes no extraneous information or inconsistencies
- Uses a variety of rhetorical devices
- Uses a variety of sentence structures
- Uses a variety of transitions to link paragraphs

Refer to the Scoring Guide for this writing task to help you understand where to focus your attention and efforts.

Prewriting

1. Reread and mark the writing prompt above to clarify the task.

2. As a class, brainstorm ideas for the class-generated essay, and create a list of possible topics.

3. With your class, choose a topic for the essay and write it here.

4. Use a prewriting strategy (such as brainstorming, quickwriting, or webbing) to generate specific ideas about the topic.

5. Create a graphic organizer (such as a Venn diagram) to compare and contrast the various elements of your topic.

6. To create an effective draft, you will need a thesis to focus the essay. A thesis is not the title of an essay (e.g., *Lunches*) or an announcement of the subject to the reader (e.g., *In this essay, I will tell you about different lunches*). Instead, a thesis statement provides the audience with the point a writer is making about the topic.

   Example: "Although they both go by the same name, lunches served at school and those brought from home are often extremely different."

   (This thesis indicates the topic of discussion and takes a position on the topic.)

   Using the sentence stem below, write a thesis statement for the sample expository essay.

   Although Rudi and Santo _____ (*topic and compare or contrast*), _____ (*compare or contrast*).

   Work together to draft a thesis statement for your class essay.

7. With your class, decide how you will organize your body paragraphs to support the thesis. Complete the graphic organizer below by choosing supporting ideas and brainstorming how you will use evidence to develop each one.

   Organizing Supporting Ideas aand Details

Supporting Idea	Evidence: Details, Examples, Facts

Drafting the Essay

One way to structure a compare-and-contrast essay is with the block pattern. Using this pattern, a writer discusses one idea or topic completely before moving on to the next idea. The essay might follow this order:
• Introduction with thesis
• Body paragraph 1: Similarities between the topics
• Body paragraph 2: Differences between the topics
• Conclusion

8. Working with your teacher and classmates, draft the introduction to your expository essay. Be sure to include the following elements:
   • **Lead,** or "hook": a quote, question, anecdote, or intriguing statement
   • **Context:** A connection between the hook/lead and the thesis
   • **Thesis:** The position of the class on the topic

9. With your class, generate an outline for the body paragraphs. Then, draft the body paragraphs on separate paper. Be sure to include the following elements:
   • **Topic sentence:** A sentence that states the main idea of the paragraph
   • **Transitions:** Words used to connect ideas (e.g., *for example, for instance*)
   • **Evidence:** Specific examples, details, and facts
   • **Commentary:** Sentences that explain how the information is relevant to the topic sentence

10. The conclusion should follow from and support your thesis. Use the following questions to guide your thinking in drafting a conclusion:
    • What did you say? (literal)
    • What does it mean? (interpretive)
    • Why does it matter? (universal)

Check Your Understanding

After you have completed this process, read over the completed expository essay that your class has created. Refer to the Scoring Guide to help determine how well the essay meets the requirements. Next, consider the following:
• Underline the thesis statement in the introduction and the topic sentence of each body paragraph.
• Does the essay have a clear purpose and audience?
• Circle the transitions. Do transitions connect the ideas being developed?
• How relevant are the examples and details we used for elaboration and support?
• Is the essay's style appropriate for the audience?
• Does the essay include precise and vivid language?
• Does the conclusion follow from the information in the essay?

Revising

Revising for Language and Writer's Craft

Rhetorical devices show ideas in interesting ways and help your ideas have a lasting effect on your reader. Examples of rhetorical devices are parallelism, analogy, and rhetorical questions.

ACADEMIC VOCABULARY
Rhetorical devices are specific techniques used in writing or speaking to create a literary effect or enhance effectiveness.

- Parallelism is using the same structure for similar parts of a sentence. Use parallelism to add balance, rhythm, and clarity to a sentence.

- An **analogy** compares two things and expresses the relationship between them. Use an analogy to explain or clarify an idea or object.

- A **rhetorical question** is either not meant to be answered or suggests a desired reply. Use rhetorical questions to emphasize an idea or to draw a conclusion from the facts. A rhetorical question may help remind your reader of a main point.

11. Rewrite at least one sentence from the class essay to add a rhetorical device, and then share your proposed revision with the class.

Another stylistic choice is **varying sentence structure**. One way to do this is by beginning a sentence with something other than the subject. For example, you could begin a sentence with a prepositional phrase or adverb. These words or phrases can be transitional. Notice that prepositional phrases and adverbs at the beginnings of sentences are usually set off with commas.

  In the afternoon, we enjoy listening to music. *(prepositional phrase)*
  Generally, the lunchroom is crowded just before the bell rings. *(adverb)*

12. Rewrite at least one sentence from the class essay to enhance sentence variety, and then share your proposed revision with the class.

Coherence refers to the logical organization of the essay and how the ideas are tied together to flow smoothly, thus making the essay easy for the reader to follow. One way to revise for coherence is to use transitional words within and between paragraphs. Another is to use varied sentence structures.

Transitional words and phrases help you move from one idea, sentence or paragraph to another.

Transitions that show comparison and contrast: *similarly, on the other hand, in contrast, different from, like, unlike, same as, in the same way, nevertheless, likewise, conversely*

Transitions that show a conclusion: *as a result, therefore, finally, last, in conclusion, in summary*

13. Make a list of transitional words and phrases in the class essay:

14. Rewrite at least one sentence from the class essay to add transitional words or phrases, and then share your proposed revision with the class.

Editing

15. After presenting your revisions to the class and hearing the suggested revisions of others, it's time to polish the final draft of the expository essay by editing for mistakes. Consider all of the elements listed in the Scoring Guide in the Language category.

ACTIVITY 3

Writing an Expository Essay with Peers

WRITING PROMPT: Think about how you get from place to place. What is your mode of transportation to school or to a friend's house? Write a multi-paragraph essay that compares and contrasts two different modes of transportation, explaining both the similarities and the differences between them (e.g., personal car versus public transportation, walking versus skateboarding). Be sure the essay:
• Presents effective introductory and concluding paragraphs
• Contains a clearly stated purpose or controlling idea
• Is logically organized with appropriate facts and details
• Includes no extraneous information or inconsistencies
• Uses a variety of rhetorical devices
• Uses a variety of sentence structures
• Uses a variety of transitions to link paragraphs

Prewriting/Drafting

1. With your writing group, reread and mark the prompt to highlight major elements of the task you are being asked to do.

2. Review the writing steps from the class-constructed expository essay and apply them to your group-constructed essay.
   • Brainstorm and choose a topic.
   • Draft a thesis that includes your topic and a position.
   • Create graphic organizers (such as the one on page 5 or a Venn diagram) to brainstorm and organize your supporting ideas and details.
   • Draft an introduction, body paragraphs, and conclusion.

Peer Review

3. You will evaluate and provide feedback for another group's essay, based on criteria established in the writing prompt and the Scoring Guide. Another group will review the work your group has done. Use the revision checklist that follows to guide your peer review.

Expository Essay Revision Checklist	
Topic	• Is the topic made clear in the introduction? Does it respond to the prompt?
Thesis	• Does the thesis statement combine the topic and the point the writer is making? • Does the thesis include elements of both comparison and contrast?
Support	• What examples and personal experiences does the writer use to support the thesis? • Does the writer include relevant details? • Is the evidence accurate and relevant to the topic?
Audience	• Who is the target audience? • Are the thesis, topic, and supporting ideas appropriate for the target audience?
Language and Style	• Does the writer use precise and vivid diction? • Does the writer use a style that is appropriate for the purpose and audience? • Does the writer use rhetorical devices and sentence variety to enhance the essay? • Does the writer use transitions to create coherence?
Conclusion	• Does the writer conclude the essay in a way that follows from and supports the ideas presented in the essay?

Revising/Editing

4. After rereading your group's draft, follow these strategies for revision:

   Adding: Are there any changes you could make to strengthen the essay? Does anything need to be reorganized or explained more clearly?

   Rearranging: What revisions should be made to rearrange the structure of paragraphs or sentences to make them more effective?

   Deleting: Are there repetitions that could be eliminated? Is there information that does not directly support the main idea?

   Editing: Are there mistakes in conventions that should be corrected before the draft can be considered polished?

5. As you revise, also consider varying sentence structure.

ACTIVITY 4
Independent Writing

WRITING PROMPT: Think about how you communicate with the people around you. Do you communicate with your friends in the same way as you do with your family? Write a multi-paragraph essay that compares and contrasts two modes of communication (e.g., texting versus face-to-face conversation; email versus formal letter writing). The essay should meet the requirements given in Activity 2.

Use the process, and revision steps from your previous activities to accomplish your task.

SCORING GUIDE

Scoring Criteria	Exemplary	Proficient	Emerging	Incomplete
Ideas	The essay • presents a topic that is focused and well developed throughout the essay • uses strategies of compare and contrast to effectively develop and explain ideas • incorporates specific and relevant facts, evidence, details, and examples to guide the reader's understanding of the main ideas	The essay • presents a topic that is clear throughout the essay • uses strategies of compare and contrast to develop ideas throughout the essay • uses facts, evidence, details, and examples to guide the reader's understanding of the main ideas	The essay • presents a topic that is unfocused and/or minimally developed throughout the essay • uses few strategies of compare and contrast to develop ideas throughout the essay • contains insufficient or vague facts, evidence, details, and examples that confuse the reader's understanding of the main ideas	The essay • lacks an appropriate topic in response to the prompt • lacks strategies of compare and contrast to develop ideas throughout the essay • contains minimal or irrelevant facts, evidence, details, and examples
Structure	The essay • leads with an effective and engaging introduction • effectively sequences ideas and uses meaningful transitions to clarify the relationship among ideas • provides an insightful conclusion that follows from and supports the explanation presented	The essay • presents a clear and focused introduction • sequences ideas and uses transitions to create coherence • provides a conclusion that connects the larger ideas presented	The essay • contains an underdeveloped and/or unfocused introduction • presents disconnected ideas and limited use of transitions • contains an underdeveloped or unfocused conclusion	The essay • contains a minimal or incomplete introduction • uses a confusing organization for evidence and ideas and/or few or no meaningful transitions • provides a minimal conclusion or none at all
Use of Language	The essay • uses a variety of sentence structures to enhance the explanation • uses precise diction that is deliberately chosen for the topic, audience, and purpose • utilizes a variety of rhetorical devices to enhance explanation • demonstrates technical command of conventions of standard English	The essay • uses a variety of sentence structures • uses appropriate diction that is appropriate to the topic, audience, and purpose • uses rhetorical devices • demonstrates general command of standard English conventions; minor errors in punctuation, grammar, capitalization, or spelling do not interfere with meaning	The essay • shows little or no variety in sentence structure • uses diction that is inappropriate at times for the topic, audience, and purpose • uses minimal rhetorical devices • demonstrates limited command of standard English conventions; errors in grammar, punctuation, capitalization, or spelling interfere with meaning	The essay • shows incorrect or inconsistent use of sentence structure • uses diction that is inappropriate for the topic, audience, and purpose • uses no rhetorical devices • demonstrates limited command of standard English conventions; multiple serious errors interfere with meaning

Narrative Writing: Short Story

Learning Targets
- Write narratives to develop real or imagined experiences or events using effective technique, relevant descriptive details, and well-structured event sequences.
- Engage and orient the reader by establishing a context and introducing a narrator and/or characters; organize an event sequence that unfolds naturally and logically.
- Use narrative techniques, such as dialogue, pacing, and description, to develop experiences, events, and/or characters.
- Use a variety of transition words, phrases, and clauses to convey sequence and signal shifts from one time frame or setting to another.
- Use precise words and phrases, relevant descriptive details, and sensory language to convey experiences and events.
- Provide a conclusion that follows from the narrated experiences or events.
- With some guidance and support from peers and adults, develop and strengthen writing as needed by planning, revising, editing, rewriting, or trying a new approach.
- Engage effectively in a range of collaborative discussions (one-on-one, in groups, and teacher-led) with diverse partners on grade 8 topics, texts, and issues, building on others' ideas and expressing their own clearly.
- Come to discussions prepared, having read or researched material under study; explicitly draw on that preparation by referring to evidence on the topic, text, or issue to probe and reflect on ideas under discussion.
- Use punctuation (comma, ellipsis, dash) to indicate a pause or break.

LEARNING STRATEGIES
Think-Pair-Share, Brainstorming, Marking the Text, Graphic Organizer, Skimming/Scanning, Visualizing, Drafting, Role Playing, Self-Editing/Peer Editing, Webbing, Sharing and Responding, Marking the Draft, Note-Taking, Adding, Reviewing the Prompt

Writing a Short Story

Do you ever wonder where writers get their ideas for stories? Story ideas are all around us. They may come from something as simple as meeting a stranger on a field trip or imagining some strange object in the sky to be a spaceship. The key to writing stories is imagination and practice, practice, practice. Writers use their own insights and observations about life, as well as their imagination, to create stories that entertain us, teach us something, or provide a combination of both.

You will work with your teacher and with your classmates to construct two model stories. You will then use these models to construct your own story.

ACTIVITY 1
Discovering the Elements of a Short Story

Before Reading
1. Think about a story you've read that you really enjoyed. What did you like about the story?

2. What are some elements that are common to good short stories?

During Reading

3. As you read "Priscilla and the Wimps," look for elements of a good story and mark the text when you find them.

My Notes

Priscilla and the Wimps

by Richard Peck

Listen, there was a time when you couldn't even go to the rest room around this school without a pass. And I'm not talking about those little pink tickets made out by some teacher. I'm talking about a pass that cost anywhere up to a buck, sold by Monk Klutter.

Not that Mighty Monk ever touched money, not in public. The gang he ran, which ran the school for him, was his collection agency. They were Klutter's Kobras, a name spelled out in nailheads on six well-known black plastic windbreakers.

Monk's threads were more . . . subtle. A pile-lined suede battle jacket with lizard-skin flaps over tailored Levis and a pair of ostrich-skin boots, brassed-toed and suitable for kicking people around. One of his Kobras did nothing all day but walk a half step behind Monk, carrying a fitted bag with Monk's gym shoes, a roll of rest-room passes, a cashbox, and a switchblade that Monk gave himself manicures with at lunch over at the Kobras' table.

Speaking of lunch, there were a few cases of advanced malnutrition among the newer kids. The ones who were a little slow in handing over a cut of their lunch money and were therefore barred from the cafeteria. Monk ran a tight ship.

I admit it. I'm five foot five, and when the Kobras slithered by, with or without Monk, I shrank. And I admit this, too: I paid up on a regular basis. And I might add: so would you.

This school was old Monk's Garden of Eden. Unfortunately for him, there was a serpent in it. The reason Monk didn't recognize trouble when it was staring him in the face is that the serpent in the Kobras' Eden was a girl.

Practically every guy in school could show you his scars. Fang marks from Kobras, you might say. And they were all highly visible in the shower room: lumps, lacerations, blue bruises, you name it. But girls usually got off with a warning.

Except there was this one girl named Priscilla Roseberry. Picture a girl named Priscilla Roseberry, and you'll be light years off. Priscilla was, hands down, the largest student in our particular institution of learning. I'm not talking fat. I'm talking big. Even beautiful, in a bionic way. Priscilla wasn't inclined toward organized crime. Otherwise, she could have put together a gang that would turn Klutter's Kobras into garter snakes.

Priscilla was basically a loner except she had one friend. A little guy named Melvin Detweiler. You talk about The Odd Couple. Melvin's one of the smallest guys above midget status ever seen. A really nice guy, but, you know, little. They even had lockers next to each other, in the same bank as mine. I don't know what they had going. I'm not saying this was a romance. After all, people deserve their privacy.

Priscilla was sort of above everything, if you'll pardon a pun. And very calm, as only the very big can be. If there was anybody who didn't notice Klutter's Kobras, it was Priscilla.

Until one winter day after school when we were all grabbing our coats out of our lockers. And hurrying, since Klutter's Kobras made sweeps of the halls for after-school shakedowns.

Anyway, up to Melvin's locker swaggers one of the Kobras. Never mind his name. Gang members don't need names. They've got group identity. He reaches down and grabs little Melvin by the neck and slams his head against his locker door. The sound of skull against steel rippled all the way down the locker row, speeding the crowds on their way.

"Okay, let's see your pass," snarls the Kobra.

"A pass for what this time?" Melvin asks, probably still dazed.

"Let's call it a pass for very short people," says the Kobra, "a dwarf tax." He wheezes a little Kobra chuckle at his own wittiness. And already he's reaching for Melvin's wallet with the hand that isn't circling Melvin's windpipe. All this time, of course, Melvin and the Kobra are standing in Priscilla's big shadow.

She's taking her time shoving her books into her locker and pulling on a very large-size coat. Then, quicker than the eye, she brings the side of her enormous hand down in a chop that breaks the Kobra's hold on Melvin's throat. You could hear a pin drop in that hallway. Nobody's ever laid a finger on a Kobra, let alone a hand the size of Priscilla's.

Then Priscilla, who hardly every says anything to anybody except to Melvin, says to the Kobra, "Who's your leader, wimp?"

This practically blows the Kobra away. First he's chopped by a girl, and now she's acting like she doesn't know Monk Klutter, the Head Honcho of the World. He's so amazed, he tells her, "Monk Klutter."

"Never heard of him," Priscilla mentions. "Send him to see me." The Kobra just backs away from her like the whole situation is too big for him, which it is.

Pretty soon Monk himself slides up. He jerks his head once, and his Kobras slither off down the hall. He's going to handle this interesting case personally. "Who is it around here doesn't know Monk Klutter?"

He's standing inches from Priscilla, but since he'd have to look up at her, he doesn't. "Never heard of him," says Priscilla.

Monk's not happy with this answer, but by now he's spotted Melvin, who's grown smaller in spite of himself. Monk breaks his own rule by reaching for Melvin with his own hands. "Kid," he says, "you're going to have to educate your girl friend."

His hands never quite make it to Melvin. In a move of pure poetry Priscilla has Monk in a hammerlock. His neck's popping like gunfire, and his head's bowed under the immense weight of her forearm. His suede jacket's peeling back, showing pile.

Priscilla's behind him in another easy motion. And with a single mighty thrust forward, frog -marches Monk into her own locker. It's incredible. His ostrich-skin boots click once in the air. And suddenly he's gone, neatly wedged into the locker, a perfect fit. Priscilla bangs the door shut, twirls the lock, and strolls out of school. Melvin goes with her, of course, trotting along below her shoulder. The last stragglers leave quietly.

Well this is where fate, an even bigger force than Priscilla, steps in. It snows all that night, a blizzard. The whole town ices up. And school closes for a week.

After Reading

4. What is the main focus of this short story?

The Elements of a Short Story

Short stories include these elements: *plot* and *conflict*, *point of view*, *characterization*, *setting*, and *dialogue*.

Plot

The plot is the sequence of events and actions that get the characters in the story from point A to point B, then to point C, and so on.

5. Use the **Plot Diagram** graphic organizer below to sketch the plot of "Priscilla and the Wimps." Include notes about the conflict in the story. The main character in "Priscilla and the Wimps" faces both internal and external conflicts. Take notes on both.

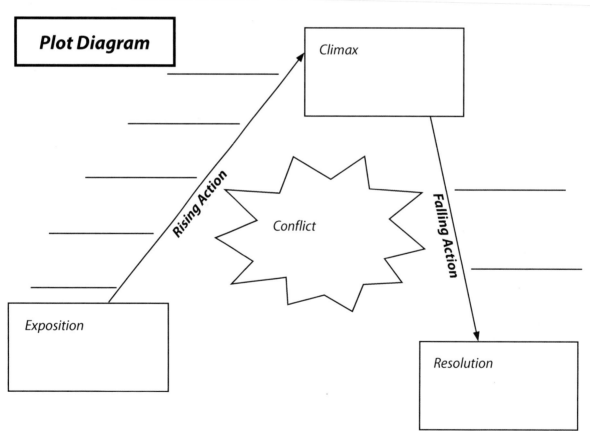

Plot Diagram

Climax

Rising Action

Conflict

Falling Action

Exposition

Resolution

Point of View

Stories are often told from either a *first-person* or a *third-person* point of view.

6. Identify the point of view Peck uses in this story. Underline or highlight the language in the story that reveals this point of view.

7. How would the story be different if the author had chosen to use a different point of view?

Characterization

Characterization is the way in which the writer reveals the personality of a character.

8. Choose either Monk or Priscilla. What does the reader know about this character? Add your findings to the **Characterization** graphic organizer below or to a graphic organizer of your own design.

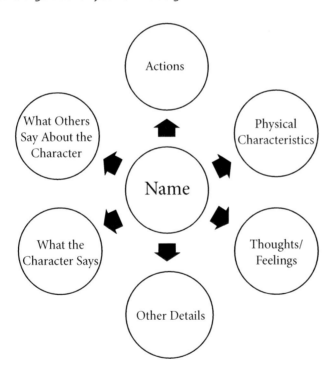

9. A character's personality or view of the world is often expressed in his or her choice of words, or voice. How realistically does the author capture the voice of teenagers? Explain. Mark the text for details that support your thinking.

Setting

Setting is the time, place, and conditions in which the story happens.

10. What is the setting for the story? Circle the words and phrases that help make the setting believable.

Dialogue

The main purpose of dialogue is communication between characters. It provides information, reveals the characters, and helps to move the story along.

11. Reread the dialogue exchanges involving the Kobra, Melvin, Priscilla, and Monk. What do the conversations reveal about the following?

   • The Kobra:

   • Melvin:

   • Priscilla:

   • Monk:

   • The plot:

12. Scan the story to find examples of figurative language. Underline them and, in the margins of the story, describe their effect on the author's style and the tone of the story. Consider whether each example suggests a certain tone, provides a description, or helps us to understand a character's attitude.

13 A *literary allusion* is a figure of speech that references a well-known person, place, event, literary work, or work of art. It calls something to the mind of the reader without describing the thing in detail. Identify some of the allusions Peck uses in his story, and consider how they affect the style and tone of the story.

Allusion	Effect on the Story

14. The author uses the literary device of foreshadowing to hint at the outcome of the story. Identify some examples of foreshadowing and explain what is being foreshadowed.

Detail from the Story	What It Foreshadows

Writing a Class-Constructed Short Story

WRITING PROMPT: Write a short story that meets the requirements listed in the Learning Targets. Refer to the Scoring Guide for this writing task—it will help you understand where to focus your attention and efforts. Be sure to

- Establish setting
- Include a clear sequence of events
- Develop a well-defined narrator and/or characters
- Choose and maintain a definite point of view throughout the story
- Include descriptive sensory details to make the setting and characters clear and interesting
- Use dialogue to show character and move the plot forward

Prewriting

Planning the Plot

1. You can find ideas for a new story by putting an original twist on a familiar story. For example, how might Melvin, with Priscilla's help, next outsmart Monk and his gang? With your class, brainstorm the possibilities of this situation. Take notes on the ideas suggested. Use the following **Plot Diagram** graphic organizer to guide your brainstorming.

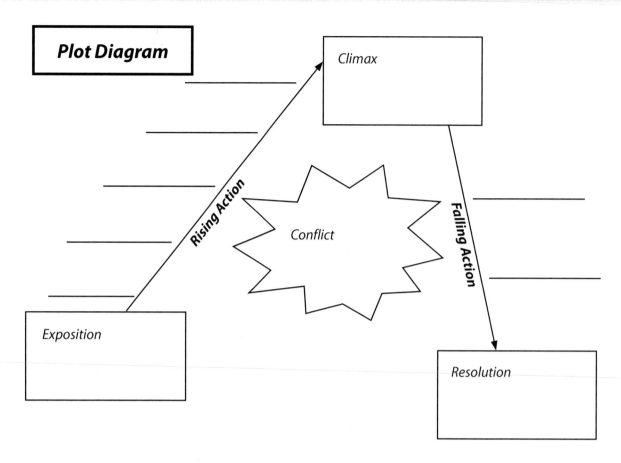

Plot Diagram

Climax

Rising Action

Conflict

Falling Action

Exposition

Resolution

Planning the Setting

2. Close your eyes and visualize a hallway or area in your school that you could use as the setting for your version of the story. Think about ways in which the setting might appeal to the senses. In a class discussion, share your responses to the questions below.

Setting

What do you **see**? (Include colors, objects, activities, etc.)	
What sounds do you **hear**?	
What textures or temperatures do you **feel**?	
What scents or odors do you **smell**?	
What might you **taste** in that setting?	

Planning and Drafting Characters and Dialogue

3. Think of how a main character in the story would change. Copy and use the **Characterization** graphic organizer used earlier to help develop this character.

4. With your class, write and role play dialogue that reveals characterization and moves the plot forward. If needed, revisit the story to see how Peck uses dialogue for these purposes.

Drafting

5. Revisit the class list of possible events in this story. Refine the rising action, climax, and resolution.

6. You and your class will now write a first draft of your class-constructed story. Use your notes and your graphic organizers to guide your writing.

Check Your Understanding

After you have drafted your short story, use the following checklist and the Scoring Guide to evaluate your story and consider revisions.

- Does the story include a clear, well-paced sequence of events?
- Are main characters believable? Do they seem real?
- Have you included descriptive, sensory details to make the setting and characters clear?
- Have you created dialogue that reveals the characters and moves the plot forward?

Revising

Revising for Figurative Language and Word Choice

7. Reread the first draft of your class-constructed story. Where might you add figurative language and allusions to other stories from books, TV programs, or movies? What effect would these achieve?

8. What tone would your class like to convey? Revise your word choices, or diction, to achieve the tone your class agrees upon.

9. Using Peck's short story as a model, find places to add foreshadowing or hints about the ending to your class-constructed story.

Revising for Transition Words or Phrases

10. Look for places in the story where there is a shift in time or location, or where a new, major event takes place. Use transition words or phrases to guide your audience without effort through the plot of the story. Here is a list of possible transition words and phrases. (Remember that transitions are usually followed by a comma.)

Shift in Time	Shift in Location	New, Major Event
Later, The next day, After he calmed down, Before that, Finally,	Meanwhile, a Across the school, At that very moment,	Suddenly, However, Because of this, For instance,

Revising for Language and Writer's Craft

Using Punctuation in Dialogue

Writers use different kinds of punctuation to help their characters and narrators sound like they are really speaking. When we speak, we often pause or break the flow of speech when we shift in tone or subject. To mirror this in writing, we can use three kinds of punctuation:

- The comma (,)
- The dash (—)
- The ellipsis (. . .)

Here is an example from "Priscilla and the Wimps":

> *"Monk's threads were more . . . subtle."*

Notice how the use of the ellipsis gives the reader a sense that the narrator paused when speaking, which gives a sense of emphasis to the descriptive word "subtle." Continued reading reveals that the narrator has used the word "subtle" ironically or mockingly. Monk's clothing is anything but simple or unremarkable!

In your writing, consider using any of the three kinds of punctuation to create the effect of pausing. Each one signals a different length of the pause or abruptness of the break. Note how the pause seems to get longer with each version of the sentence below:

> *Finally she revealed her secret crush, Calvin Johnson.*
> *Finally she revealed her secret crush—Calvin Johnson.*
> *Finally she revealed her secret crush . . . Calvin Johnson.*

In this next sentence, a writer has used a dash to indicate a break in tone in order to suggest that the last phrase is being said sarcastically:

> *Maybe we could try a day without homework—heaven forbid.*

Look over the sentences below, and rewrite them, adding punctuation to indicate a pause or break. Use each of the three kinds of punctuation at least once.

> *I wanted to take a bite of the cake so badly but I didn't.*

"I want to ask you something," said Carlos nervously.

I read and read and then read some more.

No one ever asked if I wanted to play not that I care.

David I wanted to tell you that never mind.

As you write your short stories, be sure to use punctuation to show where there is a pause or break. Use this strategy at least twice in each story. Highlight or circle instances where you do so.

Revising Punctuation to Indicate Pauses or Breaks

11   Look over the story and make sure that the story contains correct punctuation (i.e., a comma, dash, or ellipsis) to indicate a break in tone or a pause made by the narrator. There should be at least two occasions where you do this.

Editing

12. Use the model short story, "Priscilla and the Wimps," your list of the elements of a good story, and the Scoring Guide to make sure that the final draft of your class-constructed story meets the requirements of the Learning Targets.

ACTIVITY 3

Writing a Short Story with a Partner

WRITING PROMPT: Write a short story that meets the requirements listed in the Learning Targets and the Scoring Guide.

Prewriting

Generating Content

1. On separate paper, create a web and brainstorm as many twists on the class-created story as you can. You may also brainstorm other ideas for short stories that you may have.

2. Work with your partner, and take prewriting notes for your shared story.

Planning the Plot

3. Use a Plot Diagram like the one in previous activities to plan the plot of your story. Remember that your main character(s) should face both internal and external conflicts.

Planning the Setting

4. Visualize the setting. Using a graphic similar to the one you used in the class constructed short story plan how you can add sensory details to make the setting believable.

Planning Characters

5. Use a **Characterization** graphic organizer like the one in Activity 1 develop each of your characters. Add more spokes to the graphic organizer as needed, and make copies of the graphic organizers for other characters in your story.

Drafting

6. Use Peck's story and your class-constructed model story, your notes, and your graphic organizers as you and your partner draft a story opening together. You might begin in the middle of the action, or you might begin with characters in dialogue.

7. Participate with another partner pair in sharing and responding to ideas for refining your story opening. Mark the draft and take good notes so you will remember what you discussed.

8. Use your models and your notes while you and your partner continue drafting your story. Don't be afraid to modify your original plot line, as long as both partners agree.

9. Participate again in sharing and responding to ideas for refining the middle of your story. Remember to take good notes.

10. Reread the endings of your model stories. Remember that your goal is to write a story with a well-developed resolution. With your partner, draft an ending for your story.

Revising

11. Once you have drafted your story, begin to think about how you can improve your draft by revising. Use the following considerations to guide revision.

   - Reread your draft and find each detail of the setting. Consider where you might add sensory details to make the setting believable for the reader, and revise accordingly.
   - Reread your draft and consider where you might use additional dialogue to reveal information about the characters and to move the plot along. Revise and add dialogue or substitute text with dialogue. Aim for a minimum of eight sentences of dialogue.
   - Highlight figurative language used in your story. You're your partner, decide where you could add more figurative language, and take notes about the effect you hope to achieve. Improve your story by including these ideas for the best effect.
   - Identify the tone you hope to convey in a passage or in the whole story. With your partner, find where you can use more precise words, or diction, to better communicate the tone you're working toward.
   - Revisit the ending of your story. Then find places in the story to add foreshadowing that hints at the ending, but does not give it away.
   - Look for places in your story where there is a shift in time or location, or when

a new, major event takes place. Using transition words or phrases will help your audience to follow these changes in the plot of the story. Use the chart for Transition Words and Phrases used in Activity 2 as a guide.

- Look over the story and make sure that you have used correct punctuation (i.e., a comma, dash, or ellipsis) to indicate a break in tone or a pause by the narrator. Mark at least two occasions where you have done this.

Peer Review

12. Join your other partner pair in sharing and responding to thoughts and suggestions about your draft. Use their feedback on your story to help you discover additional ideas for revision. Use your notes and the feedback from your writing group discussions as you revise your short story.

Editing

13. Edit your story to eliminate errors and perfect your formatting, and prepare your work for publication.

ACTIVITY 4
Independent Writing

WRITING PROMPT: Write a short story that meets the requirements listed in the Learning Targets and the Scoring Guide. Be sure to
- Include a clear, well-paced sequence of events
- Create main characters who are believable
- Include descriptive, sensory details to make the setting and characters clear
- Create dialogue that reveals the characters and moves the plot forward
- Use correct punctuation to indicate a pause or break
- Use transitions to create coherence and guide the reader through the story

Revisit the web that you and your partner created in Activity 3. Think of twists on other stories that you know, or go through your own portfolio and brainstorm ideas for a story that you want to write. Refer to previous practice in creating short stories to help guide your short story creation. Complete your story, revise as needed, and prepare it for sharing with peers.

Make copies of and use the **Plot Diagram, Characterization,** and **Setting** graphic organizers from previous activities to help you plan your story.

SCORING GUIDE

Scoring Criteria	Exemplary	Proficient	Emerging	Incomplete
Ideas	The story • creates a detailed, vivid setting with effective use of sensory details • presents well-paced action and an intriguing story line to heighten reader interest • develops engaging and authentic characters through various forms of characterization	The story • creates a specific, believable setting using of sensory details • includes well-paced action and an engaging story line to sustain reader interest • develops interesting and realistic characters through various forms of characterization	The story • presents a vague or unbelievable setting with limited use of sensory details • contains little or no action and a story line that is incomplete or confusing to the reader • contains characters that are poorly developed or are not believable	The story • presents a setting that is not believable and provides no sensory details • contains no action and no recognizable story line • contains no believable characters
Structure	The story • leads with an opening that entices the reader • effectively sequences events that develop the conflict(s) and steadily build toward a suspenseful climax • provides an insightful ending with a clear and reasonable resolution	The story • presents an opening that grabs readers' attention • includes a sequence of events that develop the conflict(s) and build toward the climax • provides an ending that contains a clear resolution	The story • contains an underdeveloped opening that does not interest readers • presents only loosely connected events and an unfocused conflict or confusing climax • contains an underdeveloped ending with little or no resolution	The story • contains an opening that is undeveloped or lacks interest for readers • presents disconnected events and an unfocused, confusing climax • contains an ending with no recognizable resolution
Use of Language	The story • uses well-written dialogue to enhance the story line and deepen readers' understanding of characters • effectively uses literary strategies and devices to enhance and refine the story. • demonstrates technical command of conventions of standard English • uses punctuation to indicate a pause or break at several appropriate times	The story • uses dialogue to advance the story line and understanding of characters • uses literary strategies and devices to enhance the story • demonstrates general command of conventions; minor errors do not interfere with meaning • occasionally uses punctuation to indicate a pause or break	The story • uses dialogue that is incomplete or inappropriate for the story line and characters • contains few or no literary strategies and devices to present the story • demonstrates limited command of conventions; errors interfere with meaning • misuses punctuation to indicate a pause or break at appropriate times in the story	The story • uses little or no dialogue • misuses or does not use literary strategies or devices • misuses conventions to the degree that it interferes with meaning • does not use correct punctuation to indicate a pause or break

Response to Expository Text

Learning Targets

Write arguments to support claims with clear reasons and relevant evidence.

LEARNING STRATEGIES
Close Reading, Think Aloud, SOAPSTone, Marking the Text, Graphic Organizer, Notetaking, Think-Pair-Share, Brainstorming, Webbing, Outlining, Drafting, Free Writing, Rearranging, Deleting, Sharing and Responding

- Write informative/explanatory texts to examine a topic and convey ideas, concepts, and information through the selection, organization, and analysis of relevant content.
- Produce clear and coherent writing in which the development, organization, and style are appropriate to task, purpose, and audience.
- With some guidance and support from peers and adults, develop and strengthen writing as needed by planning, revising, editing, rewriting, or trying a new approach, focusing on how well purpose and audience have been addressed.
- Demonstrate command of the conventions of standard English grammar and usage when writing or speaking.
- Demonstrate understanding of figurative language, word relationships, and nuances in word meanings.
- Cite the textual evidence that most strongly supports an analysis of what the text says explicitly as well as inferences drawn from the text.
- Determine a central idea of a text and analyze its development over the course of the text, including its relationship to supporting ideas; provide an objective summary of the text.

Writing a Response to an Expository Text

The purpose of a response to an expository text is to demonstrate thoughtful understanding of the text. The writer identifies a central idea about the text and provides supporting information to communicate ideas clearly to the reader.

You will work with your teacher and with your classmates to construct two model response essays. You will use these models to help you write your own essay.

Be sure to review the Learning Targets and Scoring Guide to understand the specific requirements of this writing activity.

ACTIVITY 1

Discovering the Elements of a Multi-Paragraph Response to an Expository Text

Before Reading

Quickwrite: What do you know about writing an essay to respond to an expository text? How does a response to an expository text differ from other essays you may have written in the past?

During Reading

1. Conduct a **close reading** of Michael Lupinacci's opinion article "Jeter: Put Your Money Where Your Fans Are." As you read, mark the text for the elements of SOAPSTone and analyze the author's style and craft. This analysis will help you prepare to write a response to an expository text.

   SOAPSTone (Speaker, Occasion, Audience, Purpose, Subject, Tone) is an acronym for a series of questions to ask yourselves about a text. The questions help you analyze the central components of texts professional writers have created. SOAPSTone is also a strategy to use to plan your own writing. Review the SOAPTSTone questions below.

SOAPSTone

- Who is the **Speaker**?
  What can you infer about the speaker based on references in the text?
- What is the **Occasion**?
  What are the some of the circumstances, issues, or context (social, geographical, cultural, or historical) that might have prompted the writer to write this text?
- Who is the target **Audience**?
  To whom is this text designed to appeal or reach? Explain. What references from the text support you assertion?
  What is the **Purpose?**
  Why did the author write this text? How might the writer want the audience to think or respond as a result of reading this text?
- What is the **Subject**
  What is the writer's central idea, position, or main message about life in this text?
- What is the **Tone**?
  What is the writer's attitude toward his or her subject? Choose a few specific words of phrases from the text and explain how they support your statement.

Complete the **SOAPTSone** graphic organizer after reading the text.

My Notes

Sample Text

Jeter: Put Your Money Where Your Fans Are

by Michael Lupinacci

I teach geometry, humanities and film at a wonderful, ethnically and economically diverse public high school in New York City. In all of my classes, I push my students to develop a sense of social justice. I ask them to consider how resources can be distributed fairly in our society and what responsible citizens can do to give back. In class discussions my students often ask me difficult questions, like "Why aren't many of the wealthiest people in our country doing more?" My only answer is that many people haven't yet realized the power they have to change lives.

The truth is, my students ask a valid question. When I see the profound impact education has on the lives of my students and, by extension, the larger social fabric, I wonder why those who have so much don't do more for our kids. Earlier this year in my humanities course, I asked the students to pick a passage from "The Autobiography of Malcolm X" that got their hearts beating a little faster, and to prepare a four-minute presentation on it. Dante (not his real name) chose to discuss the revelation Malcolm had in prison about the value of being an educated person. Dante couldn't believe that Malcolm would read the dictionary for hours, especially since Malcolm couldn't read very well at that point in his life. Dante had the full attention of his 33 classmates. You could have heard a pin drop as the soft-spoken, thoughtful 17-year-old told us how he skipped class during his freshman year and nearly succumbed to the allure of crime, and how easily he could relate to Malcolm's struggle to change. When he was finished, I asked Dante if he had a dictionary at home. When he said he didn't, I brought one over and said, "Now you do." In a quiet and confused voice he asked, "You mean I can keep this?"

As I looked at Dante, I had a flashback. When I was a boy, all seven of my family members ate dinner together every night. After dinner my father and I would sit and talk. He was a New York City police officer who rarely brought his work home, but one night, when I was 10, he told me about a young boy, about my age, who was brought into the station house for stealing some clothes. My father asked the sobbing boy if he knew that stealing was wrong. The boy nodded. "Then why did you do it?" my father asked. "Because," the boy said, not looking my father in the eye, "my mother can't afford to buy me new clothes. I wear the same clothes to school every day, and the other kids make fun of me." My father said to me, "There are always going to be people out there who have more than you, but remember, son, there are always going to be those who have less." For me, being a teacher to kids like Dante is a chance to make up for the injustice suffered by the boy in my father's story.

After 10 years of teaching, I've come to accept that the role I play in my students' lives is limited—some go on to impressive colleges, some go on to prison. I've learned how to be involved with my students on a personal level while maintaining enough distance that I don't allow their difficulties to overwhelm me. Still, something about Dante's response to Malcolm X's autobiography that afternoon left me feeling restless.

On the way home from school I noticed the front page of the Daily News. Derek Jeter had just signed a $189 million contract to play baseball in the Bronx. Later that night I was just sitting, thinking. I thought about Dante and the boy who stole the clothes. Then I thought about something Plato wrote—that it is our responsibility as a society to allow children to develop their talents, regardless of the class to which they're born. There are potential doctors born every day who never have a chance to practice medicine because of neglect on our part.

It occurred to me that for any society to be great, it has to do two things. It must reward hardworking, talented people like Derek Jeter, then strongly encourage those people to share their rewards thoroughly and intelligently with their fellow citizens. I know that money won't solve all problems (give a kid a loving environment over a few extra bucks any day). But why should there be 34 students in each of my classes instead of 25, and why should the ceiling in the gym at school be too low for us to even shoot a basketball?

I'm sure that Mr. Jeter has lots of demands on his money, and my guess is that he gives a fair amount of it pretty generously. But I wonder if he realizes that if he wanted to, he could build a new public school. After all, he'll never be able to spend all of that money in a lifetime. He could change the lives of the thousands of Bronx kids who root for him and are a big part of the reason that he can make so much money doing what he loves in the first place.

Recently, I read that Andre Agassi is opening a charter school in Las Vegas. I wonder if that will help set a trend. Is it so hard to imagine that a few years from now Derek Jeter and Bernie Williams will be in the Yankee clubhouse talking about something like how to hit Pedro Martinez, when they'll turn to each other and ask, "By the way, how's your school doing?"

SOAPSTone	Analysis	Textual Support
Speaker: What does the reader know about the writer?		
Occasion: What are the circumstances surrounding this text?		
Audience: Who is the target audience?		
Purpose: Why did the author write this text?		
Subject: What is the topic?		
Tone: What is the writer's attitude toward the subject?		

Check Your Understanding

In order to create his argument, Lupinacci spends a great deal time providing us anecdotal evidence from his teaching career. Is this effective? What other evidence could he have provided to strengthen his claims?

Writing a Class Essay

WRITING PROMPT: In "Jeter: Put Your Money Where Your Fans Are," Michael Lupinacci presents his perspective on celebrities' capacity to support their local communities. In a multi-paragraph class essay, respond to this expository text, explaining Lupinacci's position and his purpose for writing this essay.

Work with your teacher and class to be sure the essay meets the requirements listed in the learning targets for writing an effective multi-paragraph response to an expository text. Refer to the Scoring Guide for this writing task to help you understand where to focus your attention and efforts.

Prewriting

1. Reread the essay and mark the writing prompt to clarify the task.

2. As a class, brainstorm ideas for the class-generated essay and create a list of possible topics below.

3. With the class, choose a main idea from the essay and write it here.

4. To create an effective draft, you will need a thesis to give focus to the essay. A thesis in a persuasive text is the writer's position or point of view on an issue. The thesis describes the writer's position, purpose, and audience. Review the information from your SOAPSTone analysis to generate a thesis. Use the frame provided to develop a working thesis.

Working Thesis: _____ wrote _____
         Author   Title
to convince _____ that _____
        Audience   Purpose/Position 1
and _____.
      Purpose/Position 2

Preparing an Outline

Topic Sentence 1

5. A topic sentence consists of a subject and an opinion that supports the thesis. The first topic sentence should support the first idea in the thesis. Review ideas generated from the prewriting, and develop a supporting topic sentence.

Support for Topic Sentence 1

6. Return to the SOAPSTone analysis to select the best facts, evidence, details, or examples to support the first position or purpose in the topic sentence. Write those examples below. Sample responses:
   - An urban teacher challenges kids to develop a sense of social justice.
   - Students question why wealthy people do not do more to support urban areas.
   - Students who have a desire to learn lack basic resources that could easily be funded by those in a financial position to lend support.
   - Responsible citizens can and should give back to struggling communities.
   - Wealthy celebrities or sports figures could do more.

Topic Sentence 2

7. Review the second position or purpose in the thesis and create a second supporting topic sentence.

Support for Topic Sentence 2

8. Choose facts, examples, details, and/or evidence to support the second topic sentence.

Drafting

Working with your teacher and classmates, begin drafting the response to "Jeter: Put your Money Where your Fans Are."

Body Paragraphs

A body paragraph has these elements:
- **Topic sentence:** A sentence that has a subject and an opinion that works directly to support the thesis.
- **Transitions**: Words or phrases used to connect ideas (*for example, for instance*).
- **Supporting information:** Specific facts and details that are appropriate for the topic, are relevant, and come from a variety of sources. Extraneous details should not be included, and the supporting information should not have inconsistencies.
- **Commentary:** Sentences that explain how the information is relevant to the thesis/topic sentence and bring a sense of closure to the paragraph.

9. Read the class sample provided below, and mark the text to identify the elements of a body paragraph.

> Lupinacci, a public school teacher in an urban community, challenges celebrity figures to invest in the future of American youth by providing fiscal support to local schools. For example, Lupinacci's position is that in order "for any society to be great," it has to "reward hardworking, talented people . . . then strongly encourage those people to share their rewards" within their local communities. Lupinacci asks his readers to consider why celebrity figures like Derek Jeter, who have the capacity to help schools meet the needs of students, have yet to do so. Society has a moral responsibility to encourage wealthy citizens to be advocates for social justice and to provide financial assistance to local schools.

10. On a separate sheet of paper, draft a body paragraph to include an appropriate quotation from Lupinacci's text. Consider using the following process to embed a quotation into the body paragraph smoothly.
   • Introduce the quote by using a transition.
   • Enter the quote and place it in quotation marks.
   • Explain the quote and how it supports your topic sentence.

   Revisit the preceding class sample, and mark the text to identify where the writer introduces the quote, uses the quote, and explains the quote.

Introduction and Conclusion
Create the introduction and conclusion. Introductory paragraphs consist of
• **A hook/lead**: Question, Quote, Anecdote, or Statement of Intrigue (**QQAS**) that is related to the topic. If you ask a question, answer it; if you use a quote, analyze it; if you use an anecdote or statement of intrigue, explain it.
• **A connection** between the QQAS and the thesis, using a TAG (title, author, genre) statement (Michael Lupinacci's article "Jeter: Put Your Money Where Your Fans Are" questions ….).
• **A Thesis statement** that makes a claim.

11. Concluding paragraphs bring a sense of closure to the essay by examining insights presented in the text and analyzing the larger meaning of those ideas. Use the following questions to guide your thinking as you craft a conclusion:
   • What did you say? (Literal)
   • What does it mean? (Interpretive)
   • Why does it matter? (Universal)

Revising

Revising for Language and Writer's Craft: Rhetorical Devices, Transitions, and Varied Sentence Structure

Now that the class essay has been drafted, consider the language used to convey ideas. A writer makes stylistic choices in language to achieve an intended effect. One stylistic choice writers often make is incorporating **rhetorical devices**. Well-chosen rhetorical devices show ideas in interesting ways and help your ideas have a lasting effect on your reader. Examples of rhetorical devices are *parallelism*, *analogy*, and *rhetorical questions*. Revise to incorporate rhetorical devices in the class essay.

- **Parallelism** is using the same structure for similar parts of a sentence. Use parallelism to add balance, rhythm, and clarity to a sentence. Examples: *I stand here today, grateful for clean air to breathe, humbled by enough food to eat, and thankful for fresh water to drink.* (parallel adjectives)
  The ecologist's briefcase held three environmentally friendly notebooks, two biodegradable writing utensils, and one recyclable water bottle. (parallel objects)
- An **analogy** compares two things and expresses the relationship between them. Use an analogy to explain or clarify an idea or object. Example: *My need to recycle is like my need for food and water.*
- A **rhetorical question** is one for which the writer expects no reply, or the writer clearly directs the reader to one desired reply. Use rhetorical questions to emphasize an idea or to draw a conclusion from the facts. Example: *Is that truly what we want for the environment? How can these facts lie?*

A **coherent** essay is one that presents ideas that tie together and flow smoothly, making the essay easy to follow for the reader. Two ways to revise for coherence are to use transitional words and to use varied sentence structures.

Review the class draft and revise to help the reader move through the essay by adding appropriate transitions.

- **Transitions to show examples:** *for example, for instance, such as, in other words*
- **Transitions to show importance**: *more importantly, most important, most of all, least, last but not least*
- **Transitions to show comparison and contrast:** *similarly, on the other hand, in contrast, different from, like, unlike, same as, in the same way, nevertheless, likewise, by contrast, conversely*
- **Transitions to conclude:** *as a result, therefore, finally, last, in conclusion*

Varied Sentence Structure
Review the draft to see where the sentence structure in your paragraphs can be varied by starting with something other than the subject. For example you can begin the sentences with a prepositional phrase or an adverb. Notice that prepositional phrases and adverbs beginning a sentence are usually set off by commas.
- ***With a little extra thought and care,*** *we can collaborate on a plan to recycle on campus.* (prepositional phrase)
- ***Generally,*** *the lunchroom is littered with trash that could be recycled.* (adverb)

Review the draft to see where you can insert word groups, such as **appositives** or **appositive phrases**, into sentences to add variety to your **sentence structure**. An appositive is a noun or noun phrase that adds information to sentences by renaming nouns (person, place or thing). Appositives and appositive phrases are located next to the nouns that they rename and are offset by a dash (a punctuation mark that indicates that more text is to follow) or commas.
- **Appositive using commas:**
Kevin, a talented pianist, inspired musicians, athletes, and artists alike to work hard to achieve their dreams.

The bat, a midnight scavenger who roams the night sky looking for food, enjoys eating mosquitoes.

- **Appositive using a dash:**
"The qualities of a writer's images—the details, colors, shapes, movement—derive from visual perception." —Harry Noden

Editing

12. Edit your class essay to be sure it is easy to understand and free of errors.

13. Reflection: What additional support do you need to write a multi-paragraph essay as a response to expository text?

Writing an Essay with Peers

WRITING PROMPT: In Lynne Isaacson's article "Student Dress Policies," she examines arguments for and against implementing school uniform policies in public schools. In a multi-paragraph response to this expository text, explain Isaacson's position and consider the purpose of her article. Be sure the essay meets the Learning Targets' requirements for writing an effective response to an expository text.

Before Reading

1. In your writing group, review and analyze the prompt.

During Reading

2. Next, read the article "Student Dress Policies." When you are done, use the SOAPSTone strategy in the graphic organizer provided to analyze the text.

Sample Text

Student Dress Policies

by Lynne Isaacson

In recent years, schools across the country have experienced violence, gang activity, and thefts of clothing and accessories. Many school boards, mindful of their responsibility to provide safe school environments for students, have implemented policies specifying dress codes or the wearing of uniforms.

As many as 25 percent of the nation's public elementary, middle, and junior high schools were expected to implement dress-related policies during the 1997-98 school year, according to the CALIFORNIA SCHOOL NEWS (March 31, 1997). Ten states allow school districts to mandate school uniforms.

My Notes

My Notes

Educators and the public are divided over the value of implementing school-uniform policies in the public schools. This Digest examines arguments for and against school-uniform policies, identifies legal considerations, and offers guidelines for implementing policies on student dress.

What are the Arguments in Favor of School Uniforms?

One of the chief benefits of school uniforms, say proponents, is that they make schools safer. Uniforms are said to reduce gang influence, minimize violence by reducing some sources of conflict, and help to identify trespassers. Parents benefit because they are no longer pressured to buy the latest fashions, and they spend less on their children's clothing.

Uniforms are also claimed to help erase cultural and economic differences among students, set a tone for serious study, facilitate school pride, and improve attendance (Cohn 1996, Loesch 1995, Paliokos and others 1996).

Proponents also say uniforms enhance students' self-concepts, classroom behavior, and academic performance (Caruso 1996).

What are the Arguments in Opposition?

Opponents contend that school-uniform policies infringe upon students' First Amendment rights to freedom of expression; interfere with students' natural tendency to experiment with their identities; are tools of administrative power and social control; offer a piecemeal approach to issues of racial and economic injustice; and may discriminate against students from minority backgrounds (Caruso 1996, Cohn and Siegal 1996).

Some believe uniforms will not erase social class lines, because policies do not apply to other items that can be used to convey status, such as jewelry, backpacks, and bikes. Uniforms may not be feasible in high schools, because older students are more independent. Others argue that it is wrong to make children's right to a public-school education contingent upon compliance with a uniform policy (Caruso, Cohn and Siegal).

What are the Outcomes to Date?

Most preliminary findings come from the Long Beach (California) Unified School District, the first U.S. public school system to require uniforms for elementary and middle school students. Before implementing its policy in September 1994, the school district required approval from two-thirds of the parents (Caruso 1996).

Long Beach Superintendent Carl A. Cohn reported that during the first year suspensions decreased by 32 percent, school crime by 36 percent, fighting by 51 percent, and vandalism by 18 percent (Cohn). At Whittier Elementary, attendance rates have risen each year since the policy went into effect, reaching a high of 96 percent (Caruso).

Schools in Chicago, Florida, Georgia, Louisiana, Maryland, New York, and Virginia have made similar claims (Caruso).

Parents have responded favorably to uniform policies. In Long Beach, only 500 parents petitioned to opt their children out of the mandate. In a national marketing survey conducted by Lands End, a Wisconsin-based clothing catalog company, respondents agreed that a uniform policy "could help reduce problems associated with dress," and most felt the price was "about the same or less than the cost of a regular school wardrobe" (CALIFORNIA SCHOOL NEWS). California requires school districts to subsidize the cost of uniforms for low-income students.

A 1996 survey of 306 middle school students in the Charleston, South Carolina, County School District found that school uniforms affected student perceptions of school climate. Students in a middle school with a uniform policy had a significantly higher perception of their school's climate than did students in a school without a uniform policy (Murray 1997).

Student reactions range from delight at not having to decide what to wear to displeasure at looking like a "nerd." It is important, therefore, to include students as well as parents in the uniform-selection process.

What Legal Issues Are Involved?

To date, most legal challenges to dress-code policies have been based on either (1) claims that the school has infringed on the student's First Amendment right to free expression or (2) claims under the Fourteenth Amendment that the school has violated the student's liberty to control his or her personal appearance (Paliokos and others 1996).

FIRST AMENDMENT CLAIMS. The clash between students' rights of free expression and the responsibility of public-school authorities to provide a safe learning environment is the central issue in the debate over dress-code policy.

In developing a ban on gang-like attire, whether through implementing a dress-code or a school-uniform policy, administrators should ask: (1) Is there a direct link between the targeted attire and disruption of the school environment? and (2) Is the prohibition specific enough to target the threatening attire without infringing on students' rights? (Lane and others 1994).

"Any dress restriction that infringes on a student's First Amendment rights must be justified by a showing that the student's attire materially disrupts school operations, infringes on the rights of others at the school, or otherwise interferes with any basic educational mission of the school" (Grantham 1994).

To defend its action if challenged in court, a state must carefully define its interest when authorizing school districts to implement mandatory uniform policies. Policy-makers must be able to document that a problem exists (Paliokos and others).

LIBERTY CLAIMS. Most challenges claiming a violation of the liberty interest have dealt with restrictions on hair length. Courts have been evenly split on whether a liberty interest exists. "Most courts that uphold the restrictions give the policy a presumption of constitutionality and place the burden on the defendant to show it is not rationally related to a legitimate school interest.... Those courts that strike down such regulations have found that schools impose unnecessary norms on students" (Paliokos and others).

What are Some Guidelines for Implementing Policies?

Lane and others offer the following advice to policy-makers: Before implementing a dress-code or school-uniform policy, be able to justify the action by demonstrating the link between a kind of dress and disruptive behavior; consult with a school attorney; and make sure the policy is enforceable and does not discriminate against racial/ethnic minorities.

In regard to uniforms, Paliokos and others recommend that policy-makers address three key questions: Are the requirements legally defensible? Do they actually restore order? Are less restrictive dress codes a better alternative? For example, policy-makers can consider five alternatives ranging from least to most restrictive:

1. Do not institute a dress code.

2. Institute a dress code that outlines general goals, and let principals and local school officials formulate and implement policy at the grass-roots level.

My Notes

3. Institute an itemized dress code that will be applied throughout the district.

4. Authorize a voluntary uniform policy.

5. Authorize a mandatory uniform policy with or without a clearly defined opt-out provision. Then policy-makers should decide whether to let schools choose their own uniforms and whether to offer financial help to low-income families (Paliokos and others).

Whichever policy is chosen, successful implementation depends on developing positive perceptions among students and parents, making uniforms available and inexpensive, implementing dress-code/uniform policies in conjunction with other educational change strategies, allowing for some diversity in uniform components, involving parents and students in choice of uniforms and formulation of policy, recognizing cultural influences, and enforcing the rules evenly and fairly.

Superintendent Cohn credits his district's success to a stable school board, supportive parents and community, resources to defend the policy, capable site administrators, and community philanthropic resources.

Resources

"California Leads Nation in Public School Uniform Use." CALIFORNIA SCHOOL NEWS (March 31, 1997): 4.

Caruso, Peter. "Individuality vs. Conformity: The Issue Behind School Uniforms." NASSP BULLETIN 8, 581 (September 1996): 83-88. EJ 532 294.

Cohn, Carl A. "Mandatory School Uniforms." THE SCHOOL ADMINISTRATOR 53, 2 (February 1996): 22-25. EJ 519 738.

Cohn, Carl A., and Loren Siegal. "Should Students Wear Uniforms?" LEARNING 25, 2 (September/October 1996): 38-39.

Grantham, Kimberly. "Restricting Student Dress in Public Schools." SCHOOL LAW BULLETIN 25, 1 (Winter 1994): 1-10. EJ 483 331.

Kuhn, Mary Julia. "Student Dress Codes in the Public Schools: Multiple Perspectives in the Courts and Schools on the Same Issues." JOURNAL OF LAW AND EDUCATION 25, 1 (Winter 1996): 83-106. EJ 527 561.

Lane, Kenneth E.; Stanley L. Schwartz; Michael D. Richardson; and Dennis W. VanBerum. "You Aren't What You Wear." THE AMERICAN SCHOOL BOARD JOURNAL 181, 3 (March 1994): 64-65. EJ 481 325.

Loesch, Paul C. "A School Uniform Program That Works." PRINCIPAL 74, 4 (March 1995): 28, 30. EJ 502 869.

Murray, Richard K. "The Impact of School Uniforms on School Climate." NASSP BULLETIN 81,593 (December 1997):106-12.

Paliokas, Kathleen L.; Mary Hatwood Futrell; and Ray C. Rist. "Trying Uniforms On for Size." THE AMERICAN SCHOOL BOARD JOURNAL 183, 5 (May 1996): 32-35. EJ 524 358.

SOAPSTone	Analysis	Textual Support
Speaker: What does the reader know about the writer?		

Occasion: What are the circumstances surrounding this text?		
Audience: Who is the target audience?		
Purpose: Why did the author write this text?		
Subject: What is the topic?		
Tone: What is the writer's attitude toward the subject?		

3. With your writing group, discuss your findings and select an appropriate prewriting strategy to generate ideas in response to the prompt. Select the best ideas from your prewriting to construct a working thesis for your essay.

4. Co-construct a preliminary outline for your essay that includes your thesis and supporting topic sentences with relevant examples and details.

Drafting

5. Review the ideas from your prewriting with your peers and co-construct a draft of the body paragraphs. Be sure to embed quotes from the article where appropriate.

6. Read your paragraphs and discuss an effective way to introduce and conclude the key ideas. Use a prewriting strategy to generate a draft that demonstrates the parts of effective introductions and conclusions.

Revising

7. Read aloud the draft to your writing group, and gather feedback based on the criteria in the goal statement for an effective response to an expository text.

8. Review the draft for coherence:
   • Discuss which transitions can be used to link ideas effectively within and between your body paragraphs. Incorporate at least two into your draft.
   • Discuss ways to revise your draft to enhance style by adding in rhetorical devices and sentence variety where appropriate.

Editing

9. Read your draft and peer edit to correct errors in grammar, punctuation, and spelling.

10. Discuss the essay's key ideas and generate a list of creative potential titles. Rank them and select one. Place a title at the top of the essay.

11. Review the Scoring Guide. Compare the essay with the Learning Targets and Scoring Guide to ensure that the essay meets all requirements. If possible, exchange your essay with another group and allow them to evaluate it against the Scoring Guide to ensure that your group's essay is successful.

ACTIVITY 4
Independent Writing

WRITING PROMPT: In Nick Mamatas' article "The Term Paper Artist," he explains his position on being hired to write papers for college students. In a multi-paragraph response to this expository text, explain Mamatas' position and consider the purpose for his article. Be sure the essay
• Presents effective introductory and concluding paragraphs
• Develops an Interpretation of an expository text and states it as a thesis
• Provides sustained evidence from the text using quotations
• Contains a clearly stated purpose or controlling idea
• Is logically organized, contains appropriate facts and details, and includes no extraneous information or inconsistencies
• Uses a variety of rhetorical devices
• Uses a variety of sentence structures and correct grammar
• Uses a variety of transitions to link paragraphs

Review the Scoring Guide to understand the specific requirements of this writing activity.

Use the class practice, process, and revision steps from previous activities to prepare for and write this essay.

The Term Paper Artist

The Lucrative Industry Behind Higher Ed's Failings

by Nick Mamatas

One great way to briefly turn the conversation toward myself at a party is to answer the question, "So, what do you do?" with, "I'm a writer." Not that most of the people I've met at parties have read my novels or short stories or feature articles; when they ask, "Have I seen any of your stuff?" I shrug and the conversation moves on. If I want attention for an hour or so, however, I'll tell them my horrible secret — for several years I made much of my freelance income writing term papers.

I always wanted to be writer, but was told from an early age that such a dream was futile. After all, nobody ever puts a classified ad in the paper that reads "Writers Wanted." Then, in the *Village Voice*, I saw just such an ad. Writers wanted, to write short pieces on business, economics, and literature. It was from a term paper mill, and they ran the ad at the beginning of each semester.

Writing model term papers is above-board and perfectly legal. Thanks to the First Amendment, it's protected speech, right up there with neo-Nazi rallies, tobacco company press releases, and those "9/11 Was An Inside Job" bumper stickers. It's custom-made Cliff Notes. Virtually any subject, almost any length, all levels of education — indulgent parents even buy papers for children too young for credit cards of their own. You name it, I've done it. Perhaps unsurprisingly, the plurality of clients was business administration majors, but both elementary education majors and would-be social workers showed up aplenty. Even the assignments for what in my college days were the obvious gut courses crossed my desk. "Race in *The Matrix*" was a fashionable subject.

The term paper biz is managed by brokers who take financial risks by accepting credit card payments and psychological risks by actually talking to the clients. Most of the customers just aren't very bright. One of my brokers would even mark assignments with the code words DUMB CLIENT. That meant to use simple English; nothing's worse than a client calling back to ask a broker — most of whom had no particular academic training — what certain words in the paper meant. One time a client actually asked to talk to me personally and lamented that he just didn't "know a lot about Plah-toe." Distance learning meant that he'd never heard anyone say the name.

In broad strokes, there are three types of term paper clients. DUMB CLIENTS predominate. They should not be in college. They *must* buy model papers simply because they do not understand what a term paper is, much less anything going on in their assignments. I don't believe that most of them even handed the papers in as their own, as it would have been obvious that they didn't write them. Frequently I was asked to underline the thesis statement because locating it otherwise would have been too difficult. But that sort of thing was just average for the bottom of the barrel student-client. To really understand how low the standards are these days, we must lift up the barrel and see what squirms beneath. One time, I got an e-mail from the broker with some last-minute instructions for a term paper — "I told her that it is up to the writer whether or not he includes this because it was sent to me at the last minute. So if you can take a look at this, that is fine, if not I understand." The last-minute addition was to produce a section called "BODY OF PAPER" (capitals *sic*). I was also asked to underline this section so that the client could identify it. Of course, I underlined everything but the first and last paragraphs of the three-page paper.

The second type of client is the one-timer. A chemistry major trapped in a poetry class thanks to the vagaries of schedule and distribution requirements, or worse, the poet trapped in a chemistry class. These clients were generally lost and really did simply need a decent summary of their class readings — I once boiled the 1000-page *New Testament Theology* by Donald Guthrie into a 30-page précis over the course of a weekend for a quick $600.

Others are stuck on their personal statements for college applications, and turn to their parents, who then turn to a term paper mill. One mother unashamedly summarized her boy and his goals like so: "[My son] is a very kind hearted young man. One who will make a difference in whatever he does. Barely can go unnoticed because of his vivacious character, happiness, and joy in life. He is very much in tune with his fortune and often helps the less fortunate." The kid planned to be a pre-med major if accepted, but was applying to a competitive college as a Women's Studies major because Mother was "told the chances of him getting into [prominent college] under less desirable subjects (as opposed to Business) was better." Finally, she explained to me the family philosophy — "Since our family places great emphasis on education, [boy] fully accepts that the only guarantee for a good and stable future can be only achieved through outstanding education."

The third group is perhaps the most tragic: They are well-educated professionals who simply lack English-language skills. Often they come from the former Soviet Union, and in their home countries were engineers, medical professionals, and scientists. In the United States, they drive cabs and have to pretend to care about "Gothicism" in "A Rose For Emily" for the sake of another degree. For the most part, these clients actually send in their own papers and they get an edit from a native speaker. Sometimes they even pinch-hit for the brokers, doing papers on graduate-level physics and nursing themselves.

Term paper writing was never good money, but it was certainly fast money. For a freelancer, where any moment of slack time is unpaid time, term papers are just too tempting. Need $100 by Friday to keep the lights on? No sweat. Plenty of kids need 10 pages on *Hamlet* by Thursday. Finals week is a gold mine. More than once the phone rang at midnight and the broker had an assignment. Six pages by 6 a.m. — the kid needs three hours to rewrite and hand in the paper by 9 or he won't graduate. "Cool," I'd say. "A hundred bucks a page." I'd get it, too, and when I didn't get it, I slept well anyway. Even DUMB CLIENTS could figure out that they'd be better off spending $600 on the model paper instead of $2,500 to repeat a course. Back in the days when a pulse and pay stub was sufficient to qualify for a mortgage, term papers — along with gigs for dot.com-era business magazines — helped me buy my first house.

Term paper work is also extremely easy, once you get the hang of it. It's like an old dance routine buried in one's muscle memory. You hear the tune — say, "Unlike the ancient Greek tragic playwrights, Shakespeare likes to insert humor in his tragedies" — and your body does the rest automatically. I'd just scan Google or databases like Questia. com for a few quotes from primary and secondary sources, create an argument based on whatever popped up from my search, write the introduction and underline the thesis statement, then fill in the empty spaces between quotes with whatever came to mind.

Getting the hang of it is tricky, though. Over the years, several of my friends wanted in on the term paper racket, and most of them couldn't handle it. They generally made the same fundamental error — they tried to write term papers. In the paper mill biz, the paper isn't important. The deadline, page count, and number of sources are. DUMB CLIENTS make up much of the trade. They have no idea whether or not Ophelia committed suicide or was secretly offed by Gertrude, but they know how to count to seven if they ordered seven pages.

I had a girlfriend who had been an attorney and a journalist, and she wanted to try a paper. I gave her a five-page job on leash laws in dog parks, and she came home that evening with over 50 pages of print outs, all articles and citations. She sat down to write. Three hours later she was rolling on the floor and crying. She tried to write a paper, instead of filling five pages. Another friend of mine spent hours trying to put together an eight-page paper on magical realism in Latin American fiction. At midnight she declared that it was impossible to write that many pages on books she had never read. She was still weeping, chain-smoking cigarettes, and shouting at me at 2 a.m. I took 20 minutes and finished the paper, mostly by extending sentences until all the paragraphs ended with an orphaned word on a line of its own.

The secret to the gig is to amuse yourself. I have to, really, as most paper topics are deadly boring. Once, I was asked to summarize in three pages the causes of the First World War (page one), the major battles and technological innovations of the war (page two), and to explain the aftermath of the war, including how it led to the Second World War (page three). Then there was this assignment for a essay class: six pages on why "apples [the fruit] are the best." You have to make your own fun. In business papers, I'd often cite Marxist sources. When given an open topic assignment on ethics, I'd write on the ethics of buying term papers, and even include the broker's Web site as a source. My own novels and short stories were the topic of many papers — several DUMB CLIENTS rate me as their favorite author and they've never even read me, or anyone else. Whenever papers needed to refer to a client's own life experiences, I'd give the student various sexual hang-ups.

It's not that I never felt a little skeevy writing papers. Mostly it was a game, and a way to subsidize my more interesting writing. Also, I've developed a few ideas of my own over the years. I don't have the academic credentials of essay experts, but I doubt many experts spent most of a decade writing between one and five term papers a day on virtually every subject. I know something they don't know; I know why students don't understand thesis statements, argumentative writing, or proper citations.

It's because students have never read term papers.

Imagine trying to write a novel, for a grade, under a tight deadline, without ever having read a novel. Instead, you meet once or twice a week with someone who is an expert in *describing* what novels are like. Novels are long stories, you see, that depict a "slice of life" featuring a middle-class protagonist. Psychological realism is prized in novels. Moral instruction was once fairly common in novels, but is now considered gauche. Novels end when the protagonist has an epiphany, such as "I am not happy. Also, neither is anybody else." Further, many long fictions are called novels even though they are really adventures, and these ersatz novels may take place in a fantastical setting and often depict wild criminal behaviors and simplified versions of international intrigues instead of middle-class quandaries. Sometimes there are pirates, but only so that a female character may swoon at their well-developed abdominal muscles. That's a novel. What are you waiting for? Start writing! Underline your epiphany.

There's another reason I never felt too badly about the job, though I am pleased to be done with papers. The students aren't only cheating themselves. They are being cheated by the schools that take tuition and give nothing in exchange. Last year, I was hired to write two one-page summaries of two short stories. Here are the client's instructions:

i need you to write me two different story in all these listed under. The introduction of the story, the themes, topic and character, please not from internet, Or any posted web sites, because my professor will know if from internet this is the reason why i' m spending money on it.Not two much words, because i will still write it back in clsss go straight to the point and write me the conclusion at end of the two story, the second story different introduction, themes, topic and character. Thank you God Bless.

At the parties I go to, people start off laughing, but then they stop.

SCORING GUIDE

Scoring Criteria	Exemplary	Proficient	Emerging	Incomplete
Ideas	The essay • contains a focused thesis • carefully incorporates well-chosen quotes • analyzes the text with insightful commentary	The essay • contains a clear thesis • incorporates appropriate quotes • analyzes the text to show in-depth thinking	The essay • contains a limited thesis • contains few, if any, appropriate quotes • contains little or no analysis or states the obvious	The essay • lacks an appropriate topic and thesis • lacks quotes or does not use them meaningfully • contains minimal or irrelevant facts, evidence, details, and examples
Structure	The essay • presents a focused inviting introductory paragraph that guides the reader • uses a variety of transitions that skillfully guide the reader's understanding • presents a fully developed concluding paragraph	The essay • presents a fully developed introductory paragraph • uses a variety of transitions to link ideas within and between paragraphs • presents an effective concluding paragraph	The essay • presents a limited introductory paragraph • contains few, or inappropriate, transitions • contains a limited or undeveloped concluding paragraph.	The essay • contains a minimal or incomplete introduction • uses a confusing organization for evidence and ideas and/or few or no meaningful transitions • provides a minimal conclusion or none at all
Use of Language	The essay • uses a skillful and effective variety of sentence types • uses clear, consistent academic vocabulary • skillfully uses rhetorical devices, transitions, and varied sentences • contains few, if any, errors in spelling, capitalization, and punctuation	The essay • uses a well-chosen variety of sentence types • uses precise and appropriate diction • uses appropriate rhetorical devices, transitions, and sentence structures • contains minor errors in spelling, capitalization, and punctuation that do not affect the reader's understanding	The essay • uses mostly simple or incomplete sentences • uses vague or imprecise words • uses few rhetorical devices or transitions, little variety in sentences • contains errors in spelling, capitalization, and punctuation that interfere with the reader's understanding	The essay • shows incorrect or inconsistent use of sentence structure • uses diction that is inappropriate for the topic, audience, and purpose • does not use rhetorical devices or transitions, does not vary sentences • shows limited command of conventions; serious errors interfere with meaning

Research Writing

Learning Targets
- Produce clear and coherent writing in which the development, organization, and style are appropriate to task, purpose, and audience.
- With some guidance and support from peers and adults, develop and strengthen writing as needed by planning, revising, editing, rewriting, or trying a new approach, focusing on how well purpose and audience have been addressed.
- Use technology, including the Internet, to produce and publish writing and present the relationships between information and ideas efficiently as well as to interact and collaborate with others.
- Conduct short research projects to answer a question (including a self-generated question), drawing on several sources and generating additional related, focused questions that allow for multiple avenues of exploration.
- Gather relevant information from multiple print and digital sources, using search terms effectively; assess the credibility and accuracy of each source; and quote or paraphrase the data and conclusions of others while avoiding plagiarism and following a standard format for citation.
- Draw evidence from literary or informational texts to support analysis, reflection, and research.
- Engage effectively in a range of collaborative discussions (one-on-one, in groups, and teacher-led) with diverse partners on grade 8 topics, texts, and issues, building on others' ideas and expressing their own clearly.
- Come to discussions prepared, having read or researched material under study; explicitly draw on that preparation by referring to evidence on the topic, text, or issue to probe and reflect on ideas under discussion.
- Demonstrate command of the conventions of standard English capitalization, punctuation, and spelling.

LEARNING STRATEGIES
Brainstorming, Think-Pair-Share, Note-taking, Drafting, Discussion Groups, Marking the Text, Annotating the Text, Graphic Organizers

Research Writing

To write reports or communicate information to others, you may need to conduct research on a chosen topic. Creating and following an organized plan for your research will help you collect appropriate information for your finished report or communication. When conducting and presenting research, it is important to follow a process that includes:
- A research plan with the topic, research question, and possible sources to be consulted
- Relevant, valid, and reliable primary and/or secondary sources
- Relevant research information recorded in notes
- Bibliographic information recorded in a standard format
- Demonstrated understanding of plagiarism and paraphrasing
- Evaluation of research results, clarifying questions, and assembled findings
- Findings organized and presented to address a specific purpose and audience

To complete this workshop, you will work with your teacher and classmates to conduct research and present your findings. You will then use these models to plan and conduct research on a topic of your choice to present to your classmates.

ACTIVITY 1

Discovering the Elements of Research Writing

Before Reading

1. Think about your previous experiences with research. In small groups, discuss the following questions. You will share your responses with the group.
   - How did you choose a topic to research?
   - What role did audience and purpose for writing play in helping you to choose a topic?
   - How did you find sources to research your topic?
   - What types of sources did you use?
   - How did you decide which sources were good?
   - How did you take notes and summarize the information you found?
   - How did you write about or present your findings?

During Reading

2 Below is a sample research presentation for your review.
   - What is the research topic? What do you think would be a good research question for this topic?
   - Circle the major idea of the research paper.
   - Underline key points of information in each paragraph.
   - Note where quotations are incorporated into the research paper. Are they used smoothly and cited correctly?
   - Look at the sources for the information presented. How do you know they are good sources? Which are primary and which are secondary sources? Which is a print source and which is electronic?

My Notes

Sample Student Text

Banning Soda in Schools— Is It Enough?

Many schools are changing. The long line of soda machines in the halls are disappearing. Bottled water is replacing Coke and Pepsi, and for a good reason. Seventeen percent of children in this country are obese. That is three times as many children as there were in the previous generation ("Childhood Overweight"). It's important to do what we can to fight obesity and poor nutrition, especially in our schools. Banning soda from schools is one step to improve this problem, but we're learning that it can't be the only one. More information is showing that banning soda doesn't do enough to really improve students' diets.

Once soda machines were removed from schools, many thought there would be a quick reduction in the amount of obese students. That is understandable, soda "accounts for more calories than any other food or beverage groups for teens between the ages of 14 to 18" (Park). However, a recent study showed that, in fact, the move has had almost no impact at all (O'Connor D1). This may be surprising, but in fact, it seems that banning soda is not enough. It's only a half-step that "removes sodas from schools but not Snapple, Gatorade, and other sugary drinks" (O'Connor D1). In fact, many young people avoid drinking sodas like Coke, but regularly drink "sports drinks and energy drinks that are not covered by the soda-only ban" (Park).

The facts are clear; more needs to be done. All beverages that contain high amounts of sugar should be removed from schools, even if this means losing the money that schools make off of their sale. More schools should be like the ones in the Eula Independent School District in Texas. There, students are told that sodas purchased outside the school are not allowed in their cafeterias ("Eula Schools").

Also, if school is the only place where young people are discouraged from drinking unhealthy beverages, it seems unlikely that we'll ever really put a stop to the obesity crisis. The study that showed students shifting to different sugary drinks also warned about other ways that students make up for school-based bans. While students who were not heavy soda users did drink less due to bans, heavy drinkers made up for the bans "with increased consumption outside of school" (Park). This is not to say that soda bans should be abandoned. Instead, we need to do more, expanding the bans to more sugary beverages and looking for ways to discourage children and teens from drinking these drinks in their free time. The country faces a genuine health crisis that is threatening our youth. This is no time for half measures.

Works Cited

"Childhood Overweight and Obesity." *CDC: Overweight and Obesity*. Centers for Disease Control and Prevention. 7 June 2012. Web. 4 April 2013.

O'Connor, Anahad. "Soda Bans in Schools Have Limited Impact." *New York Times*. 7 November 2011. D1. Print.

Park, Madison. "Are School Soda Bans Effective?" *The Chart*. CNN.com. 8 November 2011. Web. 3 April 2013.

"Eula Schools Student Handbook." Eula Independent School District. n.d. Web. 4 April 2013.

After Reading
Language and Writer's Craft: Avoiding Misplaced and Dangling Modifiers

We use modifying phrases to add information to sentences. For example:
Before the storm, *the sky was quite clear.*

The prepositional phrase "before the storm" modifies the noun "the sky," providing more information. A good way to show exactly what the prepositional phrase is modifying is to make sure the phrase is as close to that word as possible, especially in a complex sentence. Two mistakes that writers should avoid are misplaced modifiers and dangling modifiers.

Misplaced Modifiers
This error occurs when a phrase is incorrectly placed in a sentence so that it appears to modify the wrong word. Usually, this is because the modifying phrase is placed too close to that wrong word or phrase. For example:
The squirrel looked at the girl eating his acorn.

Either this scene presents an unusual snack choice, or the writer needs to revise this sentence. Here are two ways to move the modifying phrase so that it is no longer misplaced:
Eating his acorn, the squirrel looked at the girl.
The squirrel, eating his acorn, looked at the girl.

Dangling Modifiers

Like a misplaced modifier, this error occurs when a phrase is incorrectly placed in a sentence so that it appears to modify the wrong word. In this case, however, whatever the writer wanted to modify is missing from the sentence. Because of this, the modifying phrase is left "dangling." For example,

When finished with dinner, the restaurant offered a tray of desserts.

This sentence is arranged so that the phrase "when finished with dinner" modifies "the restaurant." Adding in the word the writer intended to modify clears this up:

*When **we** finished dinner, the restaurant offered a tray of desserts.*

Practice

The following sentences have misplaced or dangling modifiers. Revise them so that they can be easily understood by readers.

After reading the reviews, the movie should be very funny.

He delivered packages to the children wrapped in brown paper.

When surrounded by the wolves, his legs began to shake.

I got up and walked the dog in my pajamas.

Although stale, Bob ate the cookie.

As you conduct your own research and present your findings, both individually and with peers, be sure to look over your sentences for modifying phrases. Check for misplaced and dangling modifiers, and revise them so that your audience can understand your intended meaning.

Constructing a Research Presentation Together

1. As a class, brainstorm some possible topics for a research project that involves multiple positions. Consider a local, national, or international issue that has more than one side. It may involve a disagreement, or it may involve multiple solutions to a problem (for example, how to help solve an outbreak of hunger in another part of the world).

2. With your teacher, you and your classmates will choose a research topic, develop possible questions to guide your research on this topic, and create a research plan.

   • What topic has the class chosen to research?

   • In small groups, compose at least three open-ended questions that could be used to investigate the topic the class has chosen. Then, as a class, you will decide which questions you want to pursue.

3. To collect information about a topic, researchers use either primary or secondary sources.
   • A **primary source** is an original document that provides firsthand information about a subject. Examples: historical documents, scientific studies
   • A **secondary source** summarizes or interprets information from a primary source. Examples: history textbooks, articles about scientific studies

You will also use print and electronic sources. Consider these questions as you choose resources for your research.
• What are the benefits and drawbacks of each type of source?
• In general, why are print sources such as encyclopedias and books more reliable than Internet sources?
• Why might electronic sources be more valuable for certain topics?
• How will your topic help you determine whether primary or secondary sources, or a combination of both, will be more relevant or important to your research question?
Your topic will help determine the relevance of each type of source to your research question.

4. Use the following graphic organizer to develop a plan for conducting the class research. Decide what information you will need in order to answer your questions and what sources would best give you the information you need.

Research Plan

Looking for Expertise: What sort of journalistic sources (newspapers, magazines, news websites) might have useful information on this topic?

Looking for Expertise: What sort of government agencies might provide useful information?

Looking for Expertise: What sort of educational institutions might provide useful information? (For example, what department at a university might share information that would be helpful?)

Specific Questions to Answer	Ideas for Where to Find the Answer

Search Terms: What are specific words or phrases that should be effective when using a search engine or online database?

5. **Evaluating Online Resources**

Anyone can publish on the World Wide Web. This is both a strength and a flaw of the Internet. If you are going to use online sources, you must be aware of the differences in quality that exist among Web sites. The following is a list of standards that you should use to judge any source you use from the Internet.

The URL
- What is its domain?
  - .com = a for-profit organization
  - .gov, .mil, .us (or other country code) = a government site
  - .edu = an educational institution
  - .org = a nonprofit organization
- Is this URL someone's personal page? (Why might using information from a personal page be a problem?)
- Do you recognize who is publishing this page? If not, you may need to investigate further to determine whether the publisher is an expert on the topic.

Sponsor
- Does the Web site easily give information about the organization or group that sponsors it?
- Does it have a link (often called "About Us") that leads you to that information?
- What do you learn when you visit that link?

Timeliness
- When was the page last updated (usually this is posted at the top or bottom of the page)?
- How current a page is may indicate how accurate or useful the information in it will be.

Purpose
- What is the purpose of the page?
- Who is the target audience?
- Does it present information or opinions?
- Is it primarily objective or subjective?
- How do you know?

Author
- What credentials does the author have?
- Is this person or group considered an authority on the topic?

Links
- Does the page provide links?
- Do they work?
- Are they helpful?
- Are they objective or subjective?

6. Two ways to record important information and avoid plagiarism are **paraphrasing** and **direct quoting**. Read the following passage, and then examine the samples of each type of note taking.

"Words belong to the person who wrote them. There are few simpler ethical notions than this one, particularly as society directs more and more energy and resources towards the creation of intellectual property. In the past thirty years copyright laws have been strengthened. Courts have become more willing to grant intellectual-property protections. Fighting piracy has become an obsession with Hollywood and the recording industry, and in the worlds of academia and publishing, plagiarism has gone from being bad literary manners to something much closer to a crime.

Gladwell, Malcolm. "Something Borrowed," *What the Dog Saw*. Little, Brown and Co., New York, 2009, p. 225.

Paraphrase: Today, plagiarism is more often considered a crime than a simple act of thoughtlessness (Gladwell 225).

Direct quotation: "plagiarism has gone from being bad literary manners to something much closer to a crime" (Gladwell 225).

7. As you gather information from your sources, practice writing some information from your sources in your own words and by copying some information word-for-word to use later as a direct quotation in your research. Remember that you will have to cite your sources no matter how you present the source information.

8. If you have access to note cards, create bibliography cards for each source you consult for information. Number each of these source cards for easy reference. Then take notes on separate cards, matching the number on each note card to the number on the corresponding source card.

9. In your research, you may find useful information in a graph or a chart. Choose an example from the source materials provided for this activity, and summarize the information in written form.

10. When reviewing your research notes, you may see that you need more information. To guide additional research, generate additional questions whose answers will provide needed information. As a class, write three or four secondary questions for your research question.

11. Complete the research by collecting information on your secondary questions, and create additional note cards and bibliographic information as necessary.

12. With your class, you will prepare and execute a **presentation plan** for the information you have assembled to answer your research questions. To use the information effectively in your presentation, you will do the following:
    • Write a thesis statement that answers your research question.
    • Develop an organizational structure that provides a thoughtful presentation of your evidence, reasoning, and conclusions.
    • Read and revise your paragraphs for effective topic sentences and well-organized information.
    • Choose what you consider to be important quotations from your sources and work these smoothly into the flow of your report of information. For example: As Malcolm Gladwell notes in his essay on copyright laws, *What the Dog Saw*, "plagiarism has gone from being bad literary manners to something much closer to a crime" (Gladwell 225).
    • Revise if necessary to avoid misplaced and dangling modifiers.
    • Present your research findings, including a Works Cited page.

    Refer to the Scoring Guide for this writing task—it will help you understand where to focus your attention and efforts.

ACTIVITY 3
Creating a Group Research Presentation

1. With your writing group, go through the brainstorming process to choose a topic. Write your notes on separate paper.

2. Next, with your group, generate open-ended questions about your topic. Refine, add, and delete questions as needed. Then choose one question as your major research question.

3. Use the graphic organizer to develop a plan that explains how you will research this topic and gather information to answer the major research question.

Research Plan

Looking for Expertise: What sort of journalistic sources (newspapers, magazines, news websites) might have useful information on this topic?

Looking for Expertise: What sort of government agencies might provide useful information?

Looking for Expertise: What sort of educational institutions might provide useful information? (For example, what department at a university might share information that would be helpful?)

Specific Questions to Answer	Ideas for Where to Find the Answer

Search Terms: What are specific words or phrases that should be effective when using a search engine or online database?

4. Using the practice and modeling from the previous activities, work with your small group to find authoritative and reliable primary and secondary sources for the topic your group has chosen to research. Use the materials from the previous activity to help you judge the value of the sources that you find.

5. Once you have found, examined, and judged these sources, take notes on cards and record the bibliographic information for each source from which you have taken information. Be sure to paraphrase and use direct quotes to avoid plagiarism.

6. After finishing the first round of research on your class topic, examine and discuss the research you have done. Create additional questions that will help broaden or narrow your original topic so you can refine the topic and collect more focused information, if necessary.

7. After completing your additional research, assemble the information into a report and prepare to present it orally. Use the following process to build your report:
   • Write a thesis that answers your research question.
   • Compose paragraphs that support the thesis with the most useful and authoritative information you have gathered on the research topic.
   • Write a conclusion to your report that follows from and supports the research information presented.
   • Read and revise your paragraphs for effective topic sentences and to improve the organization of the information.
   • Use both paraphrasing and direct quotation. Cite your sources so that a reader can easily understand where the information came from by using your Works Cited page.
   • Review your writing to make sure that you do not include any misplaced or dangling modifiers.
   • Present your research findings, including a Works Cited page.

   Refer to the Scoring Guide for this writing task—it will help you understand where to focus your attention and efforts.

8. In groups, be ready to present your findings to the class.

ACTIVITY 4
Independent Research

1. For this task, follow the same process to research a topic and present it to your peers. Remember to:
   • Choose a topic that can be researched.
   • Create a major research question that limits and focuses your research topic.
   • Use the **Research Plan** graphic organizer from previous activities to create a research plan, identifying valid sources.
   • Conduct the research and take notes.
   • Examine your findings and determine additional questions for research.
   • Assemble your findings into a report for presentation to your peers.
   • Write a thesis statement and paragraph, supporting paragraphs, and a conclusion.

- Include paraphrased information as well direct quotations. Correctly cite all information so that a reader can easily understand where the information came from by using your Works Cited page.
- Revise your work to eliminate misplaced and dangling modifiers, if necessary.
- Use the Scoring Guide to review and revise your writing to correct errors in conventions.
- Present your findings in a manner directed by your teacher.

Research Plan

Looking for expertise: What sort of journalistic sources (newspapers, magazines, news websites) might have useful information on this topic?

Looking for Expertise: What sort of government agencies might provide useful information ?

Looking for Expertise: What sort of educational institutions might provide useful information? (For example what department at a university might share information that would be helpful?)

Specific Questions to Answer	Ideas for Where to Find the Answer

Search Terms: What are specific words or phrases that should be effective when using a Search Engine or Online Database?

SCORING GUIDE

Scoring Criteria	Exemplary	Proficient	Emerging	Incomplete
Development of Ideas	The presentation • communicates a focused and insightful answer to a research question • presents relevant, accurate, and credible information from multiple to guide the reader's understanding of the main ideas • effectively incorporates quotes or paraphrases the work of others while avoiding plagiarism and following standard citation format	The presentation • presents a clear answer to a research question • uses accurate and credible information from print or digital sources to guide the reader's understanding of the main ideas • uses quotes or paraphrases the data and conclusions of others while avoiding plagiarism and following standard citation format	The presentation • presents an unfocused and/or minimally developed answer to a research question • contains information from sources that may not be accurate or credible and/or confuse the reader's understanding of the main ideas • contains few quotes or paraphrasing of the data and conclusions of others, demonstrating little ability to avoid plagiarism and/or follow standard citation format	The presentation • does not present an answer to a research question • does not support main idea with information • contains no quotes or paraphrasing of others' ideas, demonstrating little ability to avoid plagiarism and/or cite basic bibliographic information
Organizational Structure	The presentation • leads with an effective and engaging introduction • effectively sequences ideas and uses transitions to clarify relationship among ideas • provides an insightful conclusion that follows from the research	The presentation • presents a clear and focused introduction • sequences ideas, and uses transitions to create coherence • provides a conclusion that connects the larger ideas presented in the research	The presentation • contains an underdeveloped and/or unfocused introduction • presents disconnected ideas and limited use of transitions • contains an underdeveloped or unfocused conclusion	The presentation • contains an underdeveloped and/or unfocused introduction • presents disconnected ideas and no use of transitions • lacks a conclusion
Use of Language	The presentation • uses diction that is deliberately chosen to the research topic • uses a variety of sentence structures to enhance the text • demonstrates technical command of conventions of standard English • consistently avoids misplaced or dangling modifiers	The presentation • uses diction appropriate to the research topic • uses a variety of sentence structures • demonstrates general command of conventions; minor errors do not interfere with meaning. • largely avoids misplaced or dangling modifiers	The presentation • uses diction that is inappropriate at times to the research topic • shows little or no variety in sentence structure • demonstrates limited command of conventions; errors interfere with meaning. • may include misplaced or dangling modifiers	The presentation • uses diction that is inappropriate to the research topic • shows no variety in sentence structure • makes frequent errors that interfere with meaning • includes misplaced or dangling modifiers

Narrative Nonfiction

Learning Targets
- Write narratives to develop real or imagined experiences or events using effective technique, relevant descriptive details, and well-structured event sequences.
- With some guidance and support from peers and adults, develop and strengthen writing as needed by planning, revising, editing, rewriting, or trying a new approach, focusing on how well purpose and audience have been addressed.
- Explain the function of verbals (gerunds, participles, infinitives) in general and their function in particular sentences.
- Engage effectively in a range of collaborative discussions (one-on-one, in groups, and teacher-led) with diverse partners on grade 8 topics, texts, and issues, building on others' ideas and expressing your own clearly.

Writing a Nonfiction Narrative

A personal narrative is a type of narrative nonfiction that provides an opportunity to take one of your experiences and share it with an audience. The experience might have been funny or sad, or it might have been an event that taught you a valuable lesson. By establishing a unique point of view and blending events and responses to the events in their narratives, writers bring their stories to life. By including reflection, writers help readers to understand the significance of the experiences they describe. As you begin writing your own nonfiction narrative, it's important to think about the impact of your experiences, and to share insights and observations about life.

To develop your skills as a nonfiction storyteller, you will work with your teacher and with your classmates to construct two model nonfiction narratives. You will then use these models to construct your own nonfiction narrative.

ACTIVITY 1
Discovering the Elements of Narrative Nonfiction

Before Reading
1. Think about a great story that you've heard several times. It might be a family story that gets repeated at get-togethers, or it might be the story of something that happened that you and your friends will never forget. Who tells this story the best? What makes his or her version of the story better than anyone else's?

LEARNING STRATEGIES:
Think-Pair-Share, Brainstorming, Marking the Text, Webbing, Graphic Organizer, Generating Questions, Drafting, Mapping, Rereading, Skimming/Scanning, Adding, Substituting, Self-Editing/Peer Editing, Sharing and Responding, Marking the Draft, Writer's Checklist

ACADEMIC VOCABULARY:
Reflection refers to serious thought about, or consideration of, an experience. In narrative nonfiction, the writer shares some of those thoughts and feelings with the reader, including what he or she learned from the experience.

2. What elements are common to good stories?

During Reading

3. Good storytelling engages the audience by presenting vivid settings, interesting characters, and carefully developed events. As you read the sample below, look for elements of a good narrative. Mark the text by putting a check mark in the margin when you find the element, and write the name of the element beside the check mark.

My Notes

SAMPLE TEXT

Universities sometimes ask professors to give a "last lecture," imagining what wisdom they would try to impart if they knew they were making their last public speech. When Carnegie Mellon asked Professor Randy Pausch to give such a lecture, he had already been diagnosed with terminal cancer and given months to live. He delivered the lecture, knowing that his three very young children, two of whom would very likely have no memories of him, would someday watch the videotape. He called the lecture, "Really Achieving Your Childhood Dreams."

excerpt from *The Last Lecture*
by Randy Pausch with Jeffrey Zaslow

It's important to have specific dreams.

When I was in grade school, a lot of kids wanted to become astronauts. I was aware, from an early age, that NASA wouldn't want me. I had heard that astronauts couldn't have glasses. I was OK with that. I didn't really want the whole astronaut gig. I just wanted the floating.

Turns out that NASA has a plane it uses to help astronauts acclimate to zero gravity. Everyone calls it "the Vomit Comet," even though NASA refers to it as "The Weightless Wonder," a public-relations gesture aimed at distracting attention from the obvious.

Whatever the plane is called, it's a sensational piece of machinery. It does parabolic arcs, and at the top of each arc, you get about twenty-five seconds when you experience the rough equivalent of weightlessness. As the plane dives, you feel like you're on a runaway roller coaster, but you're suspended, flying around.

My dream became a possibility when I learned that NASA had a program in which college students could submit proposals for experiments on the plane. In 2001, our team of Carnegie Mellon students proposed a project using virtual reality.

Being weightless is a sensation hard to fathom when you've been an Earthling all your life. In zero gravity, the inner ear, which controls balance, isn't quite in synch with what your eyes are telling you. Nausea is often the result. Could virtual reality dry-runs on the ground help? That was the question in our proposal, and it was a winner. We were invited to Johnson Space Center in Houston to ride the plane.

I was probably more excited than any of my students. Floating! But late in the process, I got bad news. NASA made it very clear that under no circumstances could faculty advisors fly with their students.

I was heartbroken, but I was not deterred. I would find a way around this brick wall. I decided to carefully read all the literature about the program, looking for loopholes. And I found one: NASA, always eager for good publicity, would allow a journalist from the students' hometown to come along for the ride.

I called an official at NASA to ask for his fax number. "What are you going to fax us?" he asked. I explained: my resignation as the faculty advisor and my application as the journalist.

"I'll be accompanying my students in my new role as a member of the media," I said.

And he said, "That's a little transparent, don't you think?"

"Sure," I said, but I also promised him that I'd get information about our experiment onto news Web sites, and send film of our virtual reality efforts to more mainstream journalists. I knew I could pull that off, and it was win-win for everyone. He gave me his fax number.

As an aside, there's a lesson here: Have something to bring to the table, because that will make you more welcome.

My experience in zero G was spectacular (and no, I didn't throw up, thank you). I did get banged up a bit, though, because at the end of the magical twenty-five seconds, when gravity returns to the plane, it's actually as if you've become twice your weight. You can slam down pretty hard. That's why we were repeatedly told: "Feet down!" You don't want to crash land on your neck.

But I did manage to get on that plane, almost four decades after floating became one of my life goals. It just proves that if you can find an opening, you can probably find a way to float through it.

After Reading

When you have finished reading, respond to the questions that follow in the space provided. Be prepared to discuss your answers with your classmates.

4. What is the main focus of this narrative?

5. Where are some moments where the writer directly tells his audience the lessons of his experience?

6. Writers often use dialogue to help capture a scene and depict the characters in a narrative, balancing direct (word-for-word, in quotation marks) and indirect (paraphrased, no quotation marks) quotes. What are some examples of direct and indirect quotes in Pausch's narrative? How does the dialogue add to the telling of the experience?

7. What are several things the narrator does that engaged you as a reader?

Check Your Understanding

8. Explain one technique Pausch uses to engage his readers. Include several examples or quotes that show how he does this.

Writing a Nonfiction Narrative as a Class

WRITING PROMPT: Consider a time when something happened to you that taught you a lesson about life, a lesson that your audience might benefit from learning. Write a narrative about your experience, encouraging your audience to think about the lesson you learned as you went through it. Consider the elements of a good story that make it engaging and entertaining. Your essay should include the learning targets for narrative essays.

Be sure to:
- Engage the reader by establishing a clear context and setting
- Use narrative techniques such as dialogue, pacing, and reflection to develop the setting, characters, and events
- Use a variety of transitions to create a clear, logical sequence
- Include descriptive techniques such as precise diction, as well as sensory and figurative language to capture actions and engage your reader
- Provide a conclusion that reflects on the significance of the experience

Refer to the Scoring Guide for this writing task—it will help you understand where to focus your attention and efforts.

Prewriting

1. With your class, brainstorm ideas for topics that are inspired by Pausch's narrative.

2. Because everyone has had different experiences, you will base your class narrative on an experience shared by your teacher. As your teacher tells you the story, take notes on the parts that seem the most interesting.

3. With the class, brainstorm a list of questions you will need answered in order to write the narrative. Use the reporter's questions (who, what, when, where, why, and how) to fill in details. Write the questions and the teacher's answers on your own paper.

4. Create a graphic organizer using the headings below to divide the story into three parts. Consider how much description and detail each will need in each part, keeping in mind that you want a narrative with pacing that will keep your audience interested. On the chart, list ideas about what you will include in each part of the story.

- **Beginning** Sets up characters, setting, and situation.
- **Middle** Explains a problem or challenge, details key events/scenes.
- **End** Solves the problem, meets the challenge, reflects on what was learned.

5. Underline examples of descriptive language (specific details, sensory descriptions, figurative language) in Pausch's narrative. Look for language that makes the story easy to visualize and interesting to read. As a class, brainstorm more precise words or language you might use to enhance the narrative the class is creating. Write these on your own paper.

6. Writers often share their feelings about an experience to help the reader understand its significance. This technique also helps the reader understand the narrator's character. Skim through Pausch's narrative, highlighting spots where he relates his own feelings and thoughts at the time of the experience. Identify places in the organizer where you might have the narrator describe a feeling or emotion. Put a question mark in those spots.

Drafting

7. With your classmates and your teacher, use your notes and your reading of the sample text to draft the **beginning** of your narrative essay. Be sure to include the following elements:
   - An engaging introductory technique (such as dialogue, a reflective statement, or a contrast)
   - Context (the situation, characters, and/or conflict that is central to the story)

Look at the first paragraphs of Pausch's narrative, and identify these elements. Then, as a class, draft the introduction to your class-constructed essay. Copy your draft below.

8. As you develop ideas in the **middle** of your narrative, focus on:
   - **Vivid descriptions** to present the setting and the events
   - **Organization** to show shifts between events, reactions, and reflections
   - **Direct and Indirect Dialogue** to help develop key scenes and to convey the attitude of the narrator and other speakers

9. With your class, use the chart to expand the characterization in the middle of your class narrative.

ACADEMIC VOCABULARY
Characterization refers to techniques for presenting and developing a character in a narrative through the narrator's own actions, thoughts, and words, as well as through introducing and describing other characters.

What the Character Says or Thinks	What Others Say about the Character
What the Character Does	Descriptions of the Character

10. Work with your teacher to draft an ending to your narrative that reflects on the significance of the story. The ending should follow from the events of the narrative, and may also link back to the story's beginning. Sometimes the writer makes the significance of the event explicit, directly stating what was learned. Other writers choose to imply the significance, suggesting rather than stating what was learned. Still others leave the significance ambiguous or unclear. What approach makes the most sense for this story, and why?

Check Your Understanding

11. Now that you have drafted the class narrative, refer to the Scoring Guide to help determine how well the narrative meets the expectations.

   a. Underline three vivid descriptions used to capture the setting, characters, or events in the narrative.
   b. Highlight sentences or phrases that present the narrator's reactions to the events and the experience.
   c. With a different color, highlight a sentence or two that reflect on what was meaningful about or learned from this experience.

Revising for Language and Writer's Craft

Verbals are verbs that work as other parts of speech. In your writing, you typically use verbs to describe actions. (I **rode** a bike.) But with a little tweaking, you can use a verb as a different part of speech, such as a noun or adjective. There are three different kinds of verbals.

   • Gerunds are verbals that work as a noun. Gerunds always end in *–ing*. They can work as the subject of a sentence: ***Jogging** is a great way to get exercise.* Gerunds can also be the object of the sentence, as in this sentence from "Getting to Zero G:" *I just wanted the **floating**.*
   • Participles are verbals that work as an adjective to describe a noun. Some participles end in *–ing*: *The **chirping** birds woke Angela.* Participles can also end in *–ed*: *Seth smiled at the **finished** painting.*
   • Infinitives are verbals that combine the word "to" with a verb, such as "to sing" or "to write."

An infinitive can work as a noun: ***To try** this hard and fail is very frustrating.* It can also work as a noun in a phrase, such as this sentence from "Getting to Zero G:" *A lot of kids wanted **to become astronauts**.*

Also, an infinitive can work as an adjective: *I have a song **to practice**.* Finally, an infinitive can work as an adverb, modifying a verb: *You must try **to relax**.*

ACADEMIC VOCABULARY
Verbals are verbs that can serve as different parts of speech, such as nouns or adjectives. Gerunds, participles, and infinitives are the three different kinds of verbals.

Using verbals allows writers to change the emphasis in a sentence and to create variety in sentence structure. For example, consider the difference between these two sentences, keeping in mind that what comes first in an English-language sentence usually receives emphasis.

> **Being weightless** is a sensation hard to fathom.

> It is hard to fathom the sensation of weightlessness.

Verbals can also be used to combine sentences, varying sentence openings and types to improve flow.

> She laughed and giggled as she wrote. She imagined how her readers would respond to the story.

> **Laughing and giggling** as she wrote, she imagined how her readers would respond to the story.

12. Write the following sentences on a separate sheet of paper.
    a. Write a sentence that uses a gerund as the subject of a sentence.
    b. Write a sentence that uses a gerund as the object of a sentence.
    c. Write a sentence that uses a participle that ends in –*ing*.
    d. Write a sentence that uses a participle that ends in –*ed*.
    e. Write a sentence that uses an infinitive as a noun.
    f. Write a sentence that uses an infinitive as an adjective.
    g. Write a sentence that uses an infinitive as an adverb.

13. Consider how you can use verbals to strengthen your class-constructed essay. Identify several sentences that could be revised to use verbals.

Editing

After making revisions with the class, polish the final draft of the narrative essay. Consider the elements listed in the Language category of the Scoring Guide, and correct any errors you find.

ACTIVITY 3

Writing a Nonfiction Narrative with a Peer

WRITING PROMPT: With input from a writing partner, write a nonfiction narrative that relates an experience that had a significant impact on you. In particular, consider how other eighth graders could benefit from hearing about this experience. As you craft your essay, think about what makes a story engaging and entertaining, and refer to the characteristics of a good narrative listed in Activity 2 on page 5.

Refer to the Scoring Guide at the end of the Workshop to help you understand where to focus your attention and efforts.

Prewriting

1. Revisit the brainstorming you did in Activity 1 in which you listed topics you might write about. Add any new ideas for topics. Choose one topic for your narrative. Work with your partner to choose a story for each of you to write. Partners should use the reporter's questions to help one another fill in the details of his or her story.

2. On paper, jot down a brief description of the characters and events involved in your story. Brainstorm sensory images and dialogue (direct and indirect) to make the setting and scenes seem vivid to your reader.

3. On another paper, make a graphic organizer like the one below and use it to plan the structure of your narrative, identifying details to add to the beginning, middle, and end of the narrative. Recall as many details of the experience as you can.

Beginning	Middle	End
Sets up the characters, setting, and situation	Explains a problem or challenge, details main events	Solves the problem, meets the challenge, learns a lesson

Drafting

4. Use Pausch's sample and your class-constructed model to help you draft an opening that engages your reader.

5. With your partner, participate in sharing and responding to refine your opening. Feedback should concentrate on:
   - What the opening does well ("I like the way you describe the classroom. Keep that up!")
   - What questions seem unanswered so far ("I'm wondering how you felt when the teacher sent you out in the hall.")
   - Ideas that you have for how your peer could improve the essay. ("Could you add some direct quotes for the scene with the principal instead of just telling me that he warned you?")

6. Use your prewriting and partner feedback to help you draft the middle section of your nonfiction narrative, describing the events in a logical order. Remember to describe how you felt at key moments. Consider where you might add moments of reflection on things you would later understand or learn. Refer to the Scoring Guide for this writing task to help you understand where to focus your attention and efforts.

7. Participate in sharing and responding to refine your telling of the incident. Make sure that your partner's feelings about the events are clear, and that the events happen in an order that makes sense. Be sure to take notes when you receive feedback from your partner.

8. Reread your narrative and consider what type of reflection to include:
   - Explicitly state what you learned from the event.
   - Imply what was learned.
   - Leave the reflection uncertain or unresolved.

Whatever approach you take, consider the impact this will have on your reader's understanding of the significance of the experience. Write your conclusion.

9. Participate in sharing and responding to refine your conclusion.

Peer Review

10. Use the Revision Checklist and the Scoring Guide to provide written feedback for your partner's narrative.

Narrative Essay Revision Checklist	
Focus	• Is the context made clear in the beginning? • Does the story stay focused on a specific event or sequence of events? • Does the experience have clear significance to the narrator?
Development	• Does the writer use a variety of techniques—characterization, dialogue, sensory details, figurative language, etc.—to create vivid descriptions in the story? • Are any details included that are unnecessary or distracting? • Does the writer clearly express his or her feelings about the events that are occurring? • Does the writer provide moments of reflection about what was learned or would be later understood?
Sequence	• Do paragraph breaks and a variety of transitions effectively signal shifts and connect events, reactions, and reflection? • Does the pacing of the story keep the reader engaged?
Conclusion	• Does the ending follow logically from the events of the story? • Is the experience's importance to the writer made clear?

Revising/Editing

11. After meeting with your partner and hearing his or her feedback, revise and edit your narrative writing. Consider adding, rearranging, or deleting to make your work stronger.

12. Edit the final version for grammar, capitalization, punctuation, and spelling. Produce a final draft of your polished work.

ACTIVITY 4
Independent Writing

WRITING PROMPT: Write a nonfiction narrative on an incident of your choice. Your narrative should have a clear focus and communicate the impact the experience had on you. Consider an experience that is important to you and that you believe would benefit other eighth graders (other than the topics already chosen). Refer to the Scoring Guide for this writing task on the next page to guide your writing. Your essay should meet the requirements listed in the Learning Targets for nonfiction narratives.

Be sure to:
- Use dialogue, pacing, and description to develop the setting, characters, and events
- Organize events, reactions, and reflections to create a clear, logical sequence
- Include a variety of descriptive techniques—careful diction, specific details, sensory descriptions, and figurative language—to engage the reader
- Use a variety of sentence openings and sentence types, including verbals, to vary emphasis and syntax
- Provide a conclusion that follows from the events of the experience and reflects on its significance to the narrator

Use the process, examples, goals, and revision strategies from your previous activities to accomplish your task, including the graphic organizers you've used previously to help you plan and revise your writing.

SCORING GUIDE

Scoring Criteria	Exemplary	Proficient	Emerging	Incomplete
Ideas	The narrative • uses a variety of narrative techniques such as dialogue (direct and indirect) and reflection to effectively tell a clear and focused story • Reflects insightfully on the meaning, importance of, or reasons for actions and/or consequences	The narrative • uses narrative techniques to tell a generally clear and focused story • reflects on the importance of the experience	The narrative • tells an unclear, unfocused story and contains little or no use of narrative techniques • contains limited reflection on the importance of the experience	The narrative • uses summary to tell a story, without using narrative techniques • contains no reflection on the importance of the experience
Structure	The narrative • provides an engaging beginning and a reflective ending that comments on the significance of the experience • uses a variety of transitions effectively to convey sequence, signal shifts, and show the relationship among events	The narrative • introduces the reader to the central incident and ends with reflective commentary about the importance of the incident • uses transitions to convey sequence and signal shifts	The narrative • contains a beginning that is unclear and/or does not directly relate to the story • presents disconnected ideas and limited use of transitions • contains an ending that is disconnected, unfocused, and/or nonreflective	The narrative • contains no clear beginning to the narrative • presents incidents without a clear sense of sequence • presents no concluding elements
Use of Language	The narrative • uses varied sentence types as well as sensory and figurative language effectively and purposefully to enhance the story • provides details, using precise words and phrases that enhance the story • effectively uses verbals (gerunds, participles, infinitives) in particular sentences • contains few or no punctuation, grammar, capitalization, and spelling errors	The narrative • uses a variety of sentence structures and sensory and figurative language to capture the action and make the story clear • generally uses precise words and phrases • uses verbals (gerunds, participles, infinitives) correctly in particular sentences • may contain minor errors in punctuation, grammar, capitalization, or spelling that do not interfere with meaning	The narrative • uses sensory and/or figurative language ineffectively or not at all • shows little or no variety in sentence structure • contains words and phrases that are repetitive and/or unclear • struggles to (or does not) use verbals correctly • contains several errors in grammar, punctuation, capitalization, and/or spelling that interfere with meaning	The narrative • uses little language that appeals to the senses • contains little variety or control in sentence length • contains diction that is vague and imprecise • includes no verbals • contains multiple and major errors in the conventions of writing that interfere with meaning

Poetry

Learning Targets

- With some guidance and support from peers and adults, develop and strengthen writing as needed by planning, revising, editing, rewriting, or trying a new approach.
- Write routinely over extended time frames (time for research, reflection, and revision) and shorter time frames (a single sitting or a day or two) for a range of discipline-specific tasks, purposes, and audiences.
- Demonstrate understanding of figurative language, word relationships, and nuances in word meanings.
- Acquire and use accurately grade-appropriate general academic and domain-specific words and phrases; gather vocabulary knowledge when considering a word or phrase important to comprehension or expression.
- Engage effectively in a range of collaborative discussions (one-on-one, in groups, and teacher-led) with diverse partners on grade 8 topics, texts, and issues, building on others' ideas and expressing their own clearly.
- Determine a theme or central idea of a text and analyze its development over the course of a text; provide an objective summary of a text.
- Determine the meaning of words and phrases as they are used in a text, including figurative language and connotative meanings; analyze the impact of specific word choices on meaning and tone.

LEARNING STRATEGIES
QHT, Think-Pair-Share, Marking the Text, Free Writing, Drafting, Discussion Groups, Sharing and Responding, Think Aloud, Guided Writing, Graphic Organizer, Adding, Deleting, Rearranging, Revising Prior Work, Self-Editing/Peer-Editing

Writing Poetry

Poetry is a type of creative and reflective writing that provides rich opportunities for recollection of past, present, or imagined experiences and thoughtful reflection. The purpose of poetry is to communicate insights, emotions, and observations through the manipulation of language.

To complete this workshop on poetry writing, you will work with your teacher and your classmates to construct two model poems. You will then use these models to write your own poem.

ACADEMIC VOCABULARY
A Shakespearean sonnet is a lyric poem with fourteen lines consisting of three four-line quatrains and a concluding two-line couplet.

ACTIVITY 1

Discovering the Elements of Poetry

Before Reading

1. Think about your own experiences with poetry. When have you read or written poetry? What kinds of things do poets write about?

2. Use the QHT chart on the following page to rate your level of familiarity with the following terms: **sonnet, speaker, tone, quatrain, couplet, enjambment, shift, syllable, meter, rhyme scheme, vivid verbs, alliteration, parallel structure, figurative language, juxtaposition, idiom, metaphor, personification,** and **simile.**

Q: Question (Unfamiliar)	H: Heard (Somewhat Familiar)	T: Teach (Very Familiar)

3. With a partner or small group, consider your prior knowledge of each of the terms in your QHT chart and discuss into which of these categories you would place them. If you can teach another word to your partner(s), do so.

4. The poem you are about to read is "Sonnet 29" by William Shakespeare. The poem is also known by its first line: "When, in disgrace with fortune and men's eyes." Based on this line, predict what you think the poem will be about.

During Reading

5. As you read the poem, mark the text by highlighting lines or words that help you understand the poem's subject or tone.

Sample Text

Sonnet 29

by William Shakespeare

When, in disgrace with fortune and men's eyes
I all alone beweep my outcast state,
And trouble deaf heaven with my bootless cries,
And look upon myself and curse my fate,
5   Wishing me like to one more rich in hope,
Featured like him, like him with friends possessed,
Desiring this man's art and that man's scope,
With what I most enjoy contented least;
Yet in these thoughts myself almost despising,
10 Haply I think on thee, and then my state,
(Like to the lark at break of day arising
From sullen earth) sings hymns at heaven's gate;
For thy sweet love remembered such wealth brings
That then I scorn to change my state with kings.

After Reading

6. When you have finished reading, respond to the following questions about the poem's **ideas, structure,** and **use of language** in the space provided. Be prepared to discuss your answers with your classmates.

   a. **Ideas:** What is the subject of the poem? Who is the speaker? What is the speaker's attitude, or tone, toward the subject? When and how does the speaker's attitude (tone) shift?

   b. **Structure:** How many stanzas and lines are there? How long are the lines? Where does the poet break the lines? How many syllables are in each line? Does the poem have a consistent rhyme scheme or meter? How do these decisions help communicate ideas and create tone?

ACADEMIC VOCABULARY
Meter refers to a pattern of stressed and unstressed syllables in a line of poetry. An **iamb** is a two-syllable metrical foot (or measure) consisting of one unstressed syllable followed by one stressed syllable. **Iambic pentameter** refers to a line of poetry with five iambic feet (which would total ten syllables). Sonnets are usually written in iambic pentameter with a specific rhyme scheme.

   c. **Use of Language:** What kinds of punctuation and capitalization does the writer use? How does the writer use imagery such as descriptive language (vivid verbs, connotative diction, sensory detail), figurative language (metaphors, similes, juxtaposition, idiom), and other sound techniques (rhyme, enjambment) to communicate ideas and create tone?

Check Your Understanding

7. **Theme** refers to the central idea or message of a poem. A poem's theme makes a comment about the subject. What is a possible theme of "Sonnet 29"?

8. Choose one line from the poem, and explain how it helps you understand the poem's tone or theme.

ACTIVITY 2

Writing a Poem as a Class

WRITING PROMPT: Work with the class to write a sonnet (or another lyric poem with a specific structured rhyme scheme.) Be sure to include:
- Imagery: descriptive and figurative language (for example: metaphor, simile, sensory detail, imagery)
- Sound techniques (for example: rhyme, alliteration, parallel structure, enjambment)
- Poetic elements (for example: quatrains, couplets, rhyme scheme, meter)

Refer to the Scoring Guide for this writing task at the end of this workshop to help you understand where to focus your attention and efforts.

Prewriting

1. Reread "Sonnet 29" and complete the chart on the following page in order to define and identify imagery (descriptive and figurative language), sound techniques, and poetic elements that you can apply to your class-constructed poem.

Figurative Language

Term	Definition	Examples
personification		
simile		
juxtaposition		
idiom		
Sound Techniques		
rhyme		
alliteration		
parallel structure		
enjambment		
Poetic Elements		
quatrain		
couplet		
rhyme scheme		
meter		
Descriptive Language		
vivid verbs		
connotative diction		
specific adjectives		
sensory detail		

2. As a class, brainstorm ideas for the class-constructed sonnet or lyric poem, and create a list of possible subjects.

3. Work with your class to make a plan for your poem's ideas, structure, and use of language by answering the following questions:

Ideas: What will be the subject of our poem? Who will be the speaker? What tone do we want to create? How and when will our tone shift?

Structure: How will we follow the structure of a sonnet? (If we choose another structure, what will it be?) How will we plan out the rhyme scheme and meter?

Use of Language: How will we include sound techniques, as well as imagery (descriptive and figurative language)?

Drafting

4. Free write to generate ideas, lines, quatrains, or couplets to contribute to the class poem.

5. Working with your teacher and classmates, create a draft by selecting and rearranging lines contributed by individual students. Make a copy of the draft on a separate page.

Check Your Understanding

After you have completed this process, read over the poem that your class has created. Refer to the Scoring Guide to help determine how well the poem meets the criteria for this assignment. Next, consider the following:
• What is the subject and theme of our class poem? What should be the title?
• Who is the speaker, and what is the speaker's tone? Does it shift? How?
• What is the structure of our poem? How did we use poetic elements such as quatrains, couplets, rhyme scheme, and meter to create this structure?
• Did we use consistent and purposeful punctuation and capitalization?
• How did we use imagery (descriptive and figurative language) to communicate ideas and tone?

Revising for Language and Writer's Craft

Comparing and Contrasting for Effect: Poets and other writers use juxtaposition and parallel structure to highlight similarities or differences among ideas. Consider how William Shakespeare uses these techniques in the second quatrain of "Sonnet 29":

> Wishing me like to one more rich in hope,
>
> Featured like him, like him with friends possessed,
>
> Desiring this man's art and that man's scope,
>
> With what I most enjoy contented least;

The phrase "with what I most enjoy contented least" is an example of juxtaposition because the "what I most enjoy" is juxtaposed to something which no longer makes the speaker feel "contented." What connotations and associations do you have with the images of enjoyment and contentment? How does this contrast contribute to the poem's tone?

6. Work with your class to generate a juxtaposition that would fit with your poem's subject and tone.

7. Two lines of this quatrain provide an example of parallel structure because they follow the same pattern, or syntactical structure. Creating this pattern sets the reader up to expect a similar thought or idea. Reread the lines below, and identify how they express similar thoughts.

   Featured like him, like him with friends possessed,
   Desiring this man's art and that man's scope

8. Rewrite at least one sentence from the class poem to add juxtaposition or parallel structure, and then share your proposed revision with the class.

Editing

9. After presenting your revisions to the class and hearing the suggested revisions of others, it's time to polish the final draft of the poem by editing for mistakes. In addition to checking that you have consistent and purposeful capitalization and punctuation, read the poem out loud to a partner to make sure the lines make sense.

ACADEMIC VOCABULARY

Effect is the result or influence of using a specific literary device. **Juxtaposition** refers to the arrangement of two or more things for the purpose of comparison. **Parallel structure** refers to a grammatical or structural similarity between sentences or parts of a sentence.

ACTIVITY 3
Writing a Poem with Peers

WRITING PROMPT: Work with a partner or small group to write a sonnet (or another lyric poem with a specific structured rhyme scheme.) Be sure to include:
- Imagery: descriptive and figurative language (for example: metaphor, simile, sensory detail, imagery)
- Sound techniques (for example: rhyme, alliteration, parallel structure, enjambment)
- Poetic elements (for example: quatrains, couplets, rhyme scheme, meter)

Refer to the Scoring Guide for this writing task to help you understand where to focus your attention and efforts.

Prewriting/Drafting

1. With your partner or small group, revisit your class brainstorming and add ideas to your list. Choose a subject and tone that is different from your class-constructed poem.

2. Work with your partner or group to make a plan for your poem's ideas, structure, and use of language by answering the following questions:

   Ideas: What will be the subject of our poem? Who will be the speaker? What tone do we want to create? How and when will our tone shift?

   Structure: How will we follow the structure of a sonnet? (If we are choosing another structure, what will it be?) What will be our rhyme scheme and meter?

   Use of Language: How will we use imagery (descriptive and figurative language), and sound techniques to convey tone and theme? How can we include purposeful and consistent use of punctuation and capitalization?

3. Free write to generate ideas or lines to contribute to the poem.

4. Working with your partner or group, create a draft by selecting and rearranging lines from each of your free writes. Make a copy of the draft on a separate page.

Peer Review

5. You will evaluate and provide feedback for another group's poem, based on criteria from the Scoring Guide. Another group will review the work your group has done. Use the Revision Checklist on the following page to guide your peer review.

Poem Revision Checklist

Ideas	• Does the poem have a title? • Is the subject clear and appropriate? • Does the poem establish a speaker? • Does the poem convey tone? • Does the tone shift? • Does the poem convey a theme (a central message, insight, or observation about life)?
Structure	• Does the poem use quatrains and couplets? • Does the rhyme scheme, meter, and overall structure appear intentional for effect?
Use of Language	• What examples of descriptive language (such as connotative diction and specific adjectives) can you find in the poem? • What examples of figurative language (such as metaphor and juxtaposition) can you find? • What examples of sound techniques (such as rhyme and parallel structure) can you find? • Is the capitalization and punctuation consistent and purposeful?

Revising/Editing

6. After rereading your group's draft, discuss these strategies for revision:

Adding: How can we communicate our tone and theme more effectively by adding descriptive language, figurative language, and sound techniques?

Consider adding language that uses juxtaposition or parallel structure.

Rearranging: What revisions should be made to rearrange the structure of our rhyme scheme and meter? Where can we use enjambment for effect or emphasis?

Deleting: Are there any words or lines that do not contribute to our meaning or tone?

Editing: Are there mistakes in conventions that should be corrected?

ACTIVITY 4

Independent Writing

WRITING PROMPT: Write a sonnet (or another lyric poem with a specific structured rhyme scheme) on a topic of your choice. Be sure to include:
• Imagery: descriptive and figurative language (for example: metaphor, simile, sensory detail, imagery)
• Sound techniques (for example: rhyme, alliteration, parallel structure, enjambment)
• Poetic elements (for example: quatrains, couplets, rhyme scheme, meter)

Refer to the Scoring Guide for this writing task to help you understand where to focus your attention and efforts.

SCORING GUIDE

Scoring Criteria	Exemplary	Proficient	Emerging	Incomplete
Ideas	The poem • presents a subject clearly and carefully • conveys a first-person point of view speaker with a complex tone that shifts as the poem unfolds • reveals an insightful theme based on reflection, personal experiences, or observations	The poem • presents an appropriate subject • conveys a first-person point of view speaker with a clear tone • reveals a theme based on reflection, personal experiences, or observations	The poem • presents an unfocused and/or minimally developed subject • conveys an unclear or undeveloped speaker, tone, and/or theme • does not have a consistent first-person point of view	The poem • lacks an appropriate subject • fails to convey a speaker, tone, or theme
Structure	The poem • uses poetic structure (quatrains and couplets) to enhance ideas • uses poetic elements such as parallel structure, rhyme scheme, and meter with sophistication for effect	The poem • uses poetic structure (stanzas and lines) • uses poetic elements such as parallel structure, rhyme scheme, and meter for effect	The poem • uses limited poetic structure and poetic elements such as parallel structure, rhyme scheme, and meter	The poem • uses minimal poetic structure and poetic elements such as parallel structure, rhyme scheme, and meter
Use of Language	The poem • uses imagery (descriptive and figurative language) with sophistication for effect • uses sound techniques skillfully to enhance tone and theme • uses consistent and purposeful capitalization and punctuation	The poem • uses imagery (descriptive and figurative language) for effect • uses sound techniques to enhance tone and/or theme • uses consistent capitalization and punctuation	The poem • uses minimal or undeveloped imagery (descriptive and figurative language) and/or sound techniques • uses capitalization and punctuation inconsistently or not purposefully	The poem • fails to use appropriate imagery (descriptive and figurative language) and/or sound techniques • uses capitalization and punctuation incorrectly and without purpose

Script Writing

Learning Targets

- With some guidance and support from peers and adults, develop and strengthen writing as needed by planning, revising, editing, rewriting, or trying a new approach. (Editing for conventions should demonstrate command of English grammar and usage, punctuation, and spelling.
- Write routinely over extended time frames (time for research, reflection, and revision) and shorter time frames (a single sitting or a day or two) for a range of discipline-specific tasks, purposes, and audiences.
- Demonstrate understanding of figurative language, word relationships, and nuances in word meanings.
- Acquire and use accurately grade-appropriate general academic and domain-specific words and phrases; gather vocabulary knowledge when considering a word or phrase important to comprehension or expression.
- Engage effectively in a range of collaborative discussions (one-on-one, in groups, and teacher-led) with diverse partners on grade 8 topics, texts, and issues, building on others' ideas and expressing their own clearly.
- Determine a theme or central idea of a text and how it is conveyed through particular details; provide an objective summary of a text.
- Determine the meaning of words and phrases used in a text, including figurative language and connotative meanings; analyze the impact of a specific word choice on meaning and tone, including analogies or allusions to other texts.

LEARNING STRATEGIES
Brainstorming, QHT, Marking the Text, Free Writing, Drafting, Discussion Groups, Sharing and Responding, Marking the Text, Graphic Organizer, Adding, Deleting, Rearranging, Revising Prior Work, Self-Editing/Peer-Editing

Script Writing

A script is a text that guides the performance of a play or film. Script writing is a type of creative writing that allows writers to share ideas and observations about life through characters, conflicts, and themes. This type of writing can use real, personal experiences as well as imagined situations. Because the ultimate purpose of a script is a dramatic performance, a scriptwriter should include stage directions or dialogue cues that provide instructions for the actors' tone, blocking, and gestures.

To complete this workshop on script writing, you will work with your teacher and your classmates to construct two model scripts. You will then use these models to write your own script.

ACADEMIC VOCABULARY
Tone refers to the attitude or emotion with which the character should deliver a line.
Blocking refers to the movement and placement of characters as they speak.
Gestures are the movement of a part of the body, especially, a hand or the head, to express an idea or meaning.

ACTIVITY 1
Discovering the Elements of a Script

Before Reading

1. Discussion: Think about your own experiences with scripts and performance. In what different ways have you seen or heard scripts performed (on stage, in film, on the radio or television)? How are scripts different from other narratives, such as novels or short stories? Have you ever seen Shakespeare plays in film or live performance?

2. Use the QHT chart on the next page to rate your level of familiarity with the following terms: **script, performance, comedy, interpretation, improvisation, prologue, chorus, setting, plot, conflict, complications, resolution, characterization, narration, dialogue, stage directions, tone, blocking, gestures, audience, mood,** and **imagery.**

Q: Question (Unfamiliar)	H: Heard (Somewhat Familiar)	T: Teach (Very Familiar)

ACADEMIC VOCABULARY

Improvisation involves composing, arranging, and acting out a scene without advance preparation. Improvisation requires actors to think up lines on the spur of the moment.

3. With a partner or small group, consider your prior knowledge of each of the terms in your QHT chart and discuss which of these categories you would place them into. In groups or pairs share understandings and definitions of those words you feel confident to teach others.

4. The script excerpt you are about to read is from William Shakespeare's *A Midsummer Night's Dream*. In this play, four characters are involved in a very complicated conflict that is summarized in the statements below.
   - Hermia and Lysander are in love.
   - Hermia's father is opposed to their marriage, so they run away together.
   - Demetrius is also in love with Hermia, so he follows them into the forest.
   - Helena is Hermia's best friend.
   - Helena is in love with Demetrius, so she follows him.
   - While all four are in the forest, a fairy puts a spell on Lysander and Demetrius so they both fall in love with Helena.
   - When Lysander and Demetrius declare their love for her, Helena thinks they are making fun of her, and that Hermia is in on the joke.
   - Hermia is shocked that Lysander suddenly seems to hate her.

   With a small group of your peers, take on the roles of the characters in *A Midsummer Night's Dream* and use improvisation to act out the situation described in the summary statements above.

During Reading

5. As you read the script, mark the text by highlighting lines or words that help you visualize what this script would look like in a performance.

Sample Text from

A Midsummer Night's Dream

by William Shakespeare

LYSANDER: Hang off, thou cat, thou burr! vile thing, let loose,
Or I will shake thee from me like a serpent!

HERMIA: Why are you grown so rude? what change is this?
Sweet love,—

LYSANDER: Thy love! out, tawny Tartar, out!
Out, loathed medicine! hated potion, hence!

HERMIA: Do you not jest?

HELENA: Yes, sooth; and so do you.

LYSANDER: Demetrius, I will keep my word with thee.

DEMETRIUS: I would I had your bond, for I perceive
A weak bond holds you: I'll not trust your word.

LYSANDER: What, should I hurt her, strike her, kill her dead?
Although I hate her, I'll not harm her so.

HERMIA: What, can you do me greater harm than hate?
Hate me! wherefore? O me! what news, my love!
Am not I Hermia? are not you Lysander?
I am as fair now as I was erewhile.
Since night you loved me; yet since night you left me:
Why, then you left me—O, the gods forbid!—
In earnest, shall I say?

LYSANDER: Ay, by my life;
And never did desire to see thee more.
Therefore be out of hope, of question, of doubt;
Be certain, nothing truer; 'tis no jest
That I do hate thee and love Helena.

HERMIA: O me! you juggler! you canker-blossom!
You thief of love! what, have you come by night
And stolen my love's heart from him?

HELENA: Fine, i'faith!
Have you no modesty, no maiden shame,
No touch of bashfulness? What, will you tear
Impatient answers from my gentle tongue?
Fie, fie! you counterfeit, you puppet, you!

HERMIA: Puppet? why so? ay, that way goes the game.
Now I perceive that she hath made compare
Between our statures; she hath urged her height;
And with her personage, her tall personage,
Her height, forsooth, she hath prevail'd with him.
And are you grown so high in his esteem;
Because I am so dwarfish and so low?
How low am I, thou painted maypole? speak;

My Notes

How low am I? I am not yet so low
But that my nails can reach unto thine eyes.

HELENA: I pray you, though you mock me, gentlemen,
Let her not hurt me: I was never curst;
I have no gift at all in shrewishness;
I am a right maid for my cowardice:
Let her not strike me. You perhaps may think,
Because she is something lower than myself,
That I can match her.

HERMIA: Lower! hark, again.

HELENA: Good Hermia, do not be so bitter with me.
I evermore did love you, Hermia,
Did ever keep your counsels, never wrong'd you;
Save that, in love unto Demetrius,
I told him of your stealth unto this wood.
He follow'd you; for love I follow'd him;
But he hath chid me hence and threaten'd me
To strike me, spurn me, nay, to kill me too:
And now, so you will let me quiet go,
To Athens will I bear my folly back
And follow you no further: let me go:
You see how simple and how fond I am.

HERMIA: Why, get you gone: who is't that hinders you?

HELENA: A foolish heart, that I leave here behind.

HERMIA: What, with Lysander?

HELENA: With Demetrius.

LYSANDER: Be not afraid; she shall not harm thee, Helena.

DEMETRIUS: No, sir, she shall not, though you take her part.

HELENA: O, when she's angry, she is keen and shrewd!
She was a vixen when she went to school;
And though she be but little, she is fierce.

HERMIA: 'Little' again! nothing but 'low' and 'little'!
Why will you suffer her to flout me thus?
Let me come to her.

LYSANDER: Get you gone, you dwarf;
You minimus, of hindering knot-grass made;
You bead, you acorn.

DEMETRIUS: You are too officious
In her behalf that scorns your services.
Let her alone: speak not of Helena;
Take not her part; for, if thou dost intend
Never so little show of love to her,
Thou shalt aby it.

LYSANDER: Now she holds me not;
Now follow, if thou darest, to try whose right,
Of thine or mine, is most in Helena.

DEMETRIUS: Follow! nay, I'll go with thee, cheek by jole.

Exit LYSANDER and DEMETRIUS

HERMIA: You, mistress, all this coil is 'long of you:
Nay, go not back.

HELENA: I will not trust you, I,
Nor longer stay in your curst company.
Your hands than mine are quicker for a fray,
My legs are longer though, to run away.

Exit HELENA

HERMIA: I am amazed, and know not what to say.

After Reading

6. When you have finished reading, respond to the following questions about the script's ideas, structure, and use of language in the space provided. Be prepared to discuss your answers with your classmates.

   a. **Ideas:** Who are the major characters in this script, and what are they like? What are their relationships to each other? What is the setting, and how can you tell? Provide specific examples from the text to show how the writer uses dialogue to develop the characters, convey complex relationships, establish a setting, and tell the story.

   b. **Structure:** What is the plot of the script, and how is it conveyed? What exposition is provided? What is the conflict? How do the complications develop the conflict? What is the resolution of the conflict?

My Notes

c. **Use of Language:** How does the dialogue provide cues for tone, blocking, and gestures? What other text features and conventions of script writing do you recognize? How does the diction and imagery create a mood and convey the humor of the situation?

Check Your Understanding

7. This script excerpt from *A Midsummer Night's Dream* does not have a narrator, but some Shakespeare plays begin with a prologue delivered by a chorus which provides background information and commentary, much like a narrator. Write several lines that could serve as a prologue in order to enhance the audience's understanding of plot, setting, character, or relationships more clearly. Explain what your prologue adds to the text.

8. This script also lacks stage directions that provide actors and directors with specific instruction on tone, blocking, and gestures. After reading the example provided, add stage directions to one line of dialogue.

Example:

HERMIA: (*Shrieking and holding her hands over her ears as if trying to block out sound*) Lower! hark, again.

ACTIVITY 2

Writing a Script as a Class

WRITING PROMPT: Work with the class to write a modern version of the script excerpt from *A Midsummer Night's Dream*. Be sure to include:

- Characterization, relationships, and setting conveyed through dialogue and/ or narration
- A plot developed through exposition, conflict, complications, and resolution
- Stage directions and dialogue cues providing instructions for tone, blocking, and gestures
- Audience engagement strategies, such as diction and imagery that create a mood and convey humor

Refer to the Scoring Guide for this writing task at the end of this workshop to help you understand where to focus your attention and efforts.

Prewriting

1. Work with other students and resources to finalize definitions of the literary terms from Activity 1. Then reread the script excerpt from *A Midsummer Night's Dream* and complete the chart that starts below in order to define and identify techniques for character, setting and plot development, as well as cues for tone, blocking, and gestures that you can apply to your class-constructed script.

Term	Definition	Examples
Character and Setting		
characterization		
character relationships		
dialogue		
setting		

Term	Definition	Examples
Plot		
exposition		
conflict		
complications		
resolution		
Performance Elements		
stage directions		
tone		
blocking		
gestures		
Audience Engagement		
diction		
imagery		
mood		
comedy		

2. As a class, brainstorm ways that you can modernize the script excerpt from *A Midsummer Night' s Dream* for the class-constructed script, and create a list of possible strategies.

3. Work with your class to make a plan for your script's ideas, structure, and use of language by answering the following questions:

Ideas: How will we transform the characters in our script? How will we establish and convey setting? What key dialogue will we need to include in order to convey setting, develop characters, and tell the story? Will we use narration such as a prologue, or rely solely on dialogue?

Structure: What are the key elements of our story's plot—beginning, middle, and end? How will we provide exposition? What is our conflict? What complications will we need to include? How will we sequence events and resolve the conflict?

Use of Language: What stage directions and dialogue cues for tone and blocking could we include? How will we use diction and imagery to create a mood? How else can we engage our audience and convey humor? What other script writing conventions will we need to follow?

Drafting the Script

4. Working with your teacher and classmates, create a draft by transforming the script excerpt. Make a copy of the draft on a separate page.

Check Your Understanding

5. After you have completed this process, read over the script that your class has created. Refer to the Scoring Guide to help determine how well the script meets the criteria for this assignment. Next, consider the following:
   - How did we convey characterization through dialogue and/or narration?
   - How did we use dialogue and stage directions to convey relationships?
   - How did we establish and convey setting?
   - Did our script have a clear beginning, middle, and end?
   - How did we provide exposition?
   - What was our conflict, and how did we resolve it?
   - How did our complications build toward a climax or turning point?
   - How did we use stage directions or dialogue cues to enhance the performance by informing tone, blocking, and gestures?
   - Did we follow the conventions of script writing, including punctuation of dialogue?
   - How did we use diction, imagery and other techniques to create a mood, convey humor, and engage our audience?

Revising for Language and Writer's Craft

FIGURATIVE LANGUAGE: Using similes, metaphors, and hyperbole can help convey emotions and humor in a script. Consider how Shakespeare uses figurative language in Lysander's opening line of dialogue at the beginning of the script excerpt:

LYSANDER: Hang off, thou cat, thou burr! vile thing, let loose,
Or I will shake thee from me like a serpent!

6. Lysander uses metaphors when he refers to Hermia as a cat and a burr. What do these comparisons say about how he feels about Hermia?

7. Lysander uses a simile when he says he will shake Hermia from him like a serpent. What does this comparison say about how he feels about Hermia?

8. Find another line of dialogue that uses metaphor or simile and explain its effect.

9. Lysander's exaggerated disgust creates hyperbole that enhances the humor of this scene by contrasting his feelings of revulsion with Hermia's confusion as she tries to remind him that he loves her. Find another line of dialogue that uses hyperbole and explain how it enhances the humor of the scene.

10. Rewrite at least one line of dialogue from the class script to add figurative language for effect, and then share your proposed revision with the class.

Editing

11. After presenting your revisions to the class and hearing the suggested revisions of others, it's time to polish the final draft of the script by editing for mistakes. In addition to checking that you have followed proper script conventions, read the script out loud to a partner to make sure the lines make sense.

ACTIVITY 3
Writing a Script with Peers

WRITING PROMPT: Work with a partner or small group to write a modern version of a different script excerpt from *A Midsummer Night's Dream*. Be sure to include:

- Characterization, relationships, and setting conveyed through dialogue and/ or narration
- A plot developed through exposition, conflict, complications, and resolution
- Stage directions and dialogue cues providing instructions for tone, blocking, and gestures
- Audience engagement strategies, such as diction and imagery that create a mood and convey humor

Refer to the Scoring Guide for this writing task to help you understand where to focus your attention and efforts.

My Notes

Prewriting/Drafting

1. With your partner or small group, read the script excerpt from A Midsummer Night's Dream below. This scene is excerpted from earlier in the play, when Demetrius is following Hermia and Lysander into the woods because he wants to marry Hermia. Helena pursues him in an effort to convince him to give up on Hermia and love her instead.

Mark the text with ideas for how you could transform the text into a modern version. Include suggestions for transforming dialogue and adding stage directions.

DEMETRIUS: I love thee not, therefore pursue me not.
Where is Lysander and fair Hermia?
The one I'll slay, the other slayeth me.
Thou told'st me they were stolen unto this wood;
And here am I, and wode within this wood,
Because I cannot meet my Hermia.
Hence, get thee gone, and follow me no more.

HELENA: You draw me, you hard-hearted adamant;
But yet you draw not iron, for my heart
Is true as steel: leave you your power to draw,
And I shall have no power to follow you.

DEMETRIUS: Do I entice you? do I speak you fair?
Or, rather, do I not in plainest truth
Tell you, I do not, nor I cannot love you?

HELENA: And even for that do I love you the more.
I am your spaniel; and, Demetrius,
The more you beat me, I will fawn on you:
Use me but as your spaniel, spurn me, strike me,
Neglect me, lose me; only give me leave,
Unworthy as I am, to follow you.
What worser place can I beg in your love,—
And yet a place of high respect with me,—
Than to be used as you use your dog?

DEMETRIUS: Tempt not too much the hatred of my spirit;
For I am sick when I do look on thee.

HELENA: And I am sick when I look not on you.

DEMETRIUS: You do impeach your modesty too much,
To leave the city and commit yourself
Into the hands of one that loves you not;
To trust the opportunity of night
And the ill counsel of a desert place
With the rich worth of your virginity.

HELENA: Your virtue is my privilege: for that
It is not night when I do see your face,
Therefore I think I am not in the night;
Nor doth this wood lack worlds of company,
For you in my respect are all the world:
Then how can it be said I am alone,
When all the world is here to look on me?

DEMETRIUS: I'll run from thee and hide me in the brakes,
And leave thee to the mercy of wild beasts.

HELENA: The wildest hath not such a heart as you.
Run when you will, the story shall be changed:
Apollo flies, and Daphne holds the chase;
The dove pursues the griffin; the mild hind
Makes speed to catch the tiger; bootless speed,
When cowardice pursues and valour flies.

DEMETRIUS: I will not stay thy questions; let me go:
Or, if thou follow me, do not believe
But I shall do thee mischief in the wood.

HELENA: Ay, in the temple, in the town, the field,
You do me mischief. Fie, Demetrius!
Your wrongs do set a scandal on my sex:
We cannot fight for love, as men may do;
We should be wood and were not made to woo.

Exit DEMETRIUS

I'll follow thee and make a heaven of hell,
To die upon the hand I love so well.

Exit HELENA

2. Work with your partner or group to make a plan for your script's ideas, structure, and use of language by answering the following questions:

   Ideas: How will we transform the characters in our script? How will we establish and convey setting? What key dialogue will we need to include in order to convey setting, develop characters, and tell the story? Will we use narration such as a prologue, or rely solely on dialogue?

   Structure: What are the key elements of our story's plot—beginning, middle, and end? How will we provide exposition? What is our conflict? What complications will we need to include? How will we sequence events and resolve the conflict?

   Use of Language: What stage directions and dialogue cues for tone, blocking, and gestures could we include? How will we use diction and imagery to create a mood? How else can we engage our audience and convey humor? What other script writing conventions will we need to follow?

3. Working with your partner or group, create a draft by transforming this scene into a script. Make a copy of the draft on a separate page.

Peer Review

4. You will evaluate and provide feedback for another group's script, based on criteria from the Scoring Guide. Another group will review the work your group has done. Use the Revision Checklist that follows to guide your peer review.

Script Revision Checklist	
Ideas	• Does the script have a title? • Does the script convey an interesting story based on the scene from *A Midsummer Night's Dream*? • Are the characters complex and believable? • Can you understand the characters' relationships? • Is the setting conveyed clearly through dialogue or narration? • Does the script use effective dialogue? • Does any narration used seem needed to tell the story?
Structure	• Does the script have a beginning, middle, and end? • Does the script have a clear conflict? What is it? • Does the script provide sufficient exposition or background information? • Does the script include complications that build toward a climax or turning point? • Does the script include a resolution?
Use of Language	• Does the script use enough dialogue cues or stage directions that you can visualize the performance? • Are there enough cues for actors to understand the intended tone, blocking, and gestures for their lines? • What kind of mood does the script create? • What techniques, such as diction or imagery, create the mood? • Does the script follow script conventions? • Is figurative language used to engage the audience and convey humor?

Revising/Editing

5. After rereading your group's draft, discuss these strategies for revision:

Adding: How can we communicate our tone and meaning more effectively by using script conventions?

Consider adding figurative language such as **similes, metaphors,** and **hyperbole.**

Rearranging: What revisions should be made to rearrange the sequence of events so that our complications build toward a climax and resolution?

Deleting: Are there any lines of dialogue or narration that would distract or fail to engage our audience?

Editing: Are there mistakes in conventions that should be corrected?

Independent Writing

WRITING PROMPT: Write a modern version of a script excerpt from *A Midsummer Night's Dream* or another Shakespeare play. Be sure to include:

- Characterization, relationships, and setting conveyed through dialogue and/ or narration
- A plot developed through exposition, conflict, complications, and resolution
- Stage directions and dialogue cues providing instructions for tone, blocking, and gestures
- Audience engagement strategies, such as diction and imagery that create a mood and convey humor

Refer to the Scoring Guide for this writing task to help you understand where to focus your attention and efforts.

SCORING GUIDE

Scoring Criteria	Exemplary	Proficient	Emerging	Incomplete
Ideas	The script • develops complex, believable characters and conveys their relationships through a variety of characterization strategies • uses dialogue and/or narration effectively to develop character and convey setting and other story elements	The script • develops characters and conveys their relationships through a variety of characterization strategies • uses dialogue and/or narration to develop character and convey setting and other story elements	The script • presents undeveloped characters, relationships and/or setting • uses dialogue and/or narration ineffectively	The script • lacks characters and/or setting • does not include dialogue and/or narration
Structure	The script • communicates a clear beginning, middle and end • includes a compelling conflict, complications, and logical resolution • provides exposition and complications that build toward a climax or turning point in a logical sequence of events	The script • has a beginning, middle, and end • includes a conflict, complications, and resolution • provides exposition and complications	The script • has an incomplete sequence of events • has a minimal conflict, complications and/or resolution • provides insufficient exposition and/or complications	The script • lacks a sequence of events • fails to include a conflict, complications and/or resolution • does not provide exposition and/or complications
Use of Language	The script • uses stage directions and dialogue cues consistently to communicate instructions for performance • creates and sustains an engaging mood through a variety of techniques, including diction and imagery • uses script conventions effectively to convey meaning, tone and humor	The script • uses stage directions and dialogue cues to communicate instructions for performance • creates a mood • uses script conventions to convey meaning, tone and humor	The script • uses minimal stage directions and/or dialogue cues • creates an underdeveloped or inappropriate mood • uses script conventions inconsistently	The script • fails to use stage directions and/or dialogue cues • lacks a mood • does not use script conventions

Procedural Texts: Business Letters

Learning Targets
- Produce clear and coherent writing in which the development, organization, and style are appropriate to task, purpose, and audience.
- With some guidance and support from peers and adults, develop and strengthen writing as needed by planning, revising, editing, rewriting, or trying a new approach, focusing on how well purpose and audience have been addressed.
- Demonstrate command of the conventions of standard English grammar and usage when writing or speaking.
- Demonstrate command of the conventions of standard English capitalization, punctuation, and spelling when writing.
- Use knowledge of language and its conventions when writing, speaking, reading, or listening.
- Engage effectively in a range of collaborative discussions (one on one, in groups, and teacher-led) with diverse partners on *grade 8 topics*, *texts*, *and issues*, building on others' ideas and expressing your own clearly.

Writing a Business Letter

Letters can be used for a variety of purposes ranging from conveying information to maintaining personal relationships. Letters can be either formal or informal. Much like other modes of writing, there are established conventions and processes for writing letters.

To complete this workshop on writing a business letter, you will work with your teacher and with your classmates to construct two model letters. You will then use these models to write your own letter.

ACTIVITY 1

Discovering the Elements of a Business Letter

Before Reading

1. Discussion: Business letters are often used to make requests of various kinds. A business letter may be written to inquire about employment, to request information, or complain about a product. Discuss a time when you or someone you know has sent a formal letter to a company or business and received something in return.

During Reading

2. The following business letter sample represents a formal letter sent as an offer of services from one company to another. The common elements of a formal or business letter are
   - Date
   - Sender's address
   - Inside address (the address of the recipient)
   - Salutation
   - Body
   - Closing
   - Signature

As you read this letter with your class, mark each element with the appropriate label from the list above. In addition, highlight the purpose of the letter and the details of the request.

LEARNING STRATEGIES
Activate Prior Knowledge, Shared Reading, Marking the Text, Think-Pair-Share, Graphic Organizer, Summarizing, Brainstorming, Drafting, Sharing and Responding

ACADEMIC VOCABULARY
A business letter is a formal communication from one party to another. Business letters are written for many purposes, such as requesting information or action from another party, ordering products from a supplier, replying to a request, or expressing an opinion. Business letters produce a permanent written record and may be taken more seriously by the recipient than other forms of communication.

My Notes

Sample Text

Dreamtime Movies Ltd
54 Oxford Road
Valleyview, WA 98765

February 24, 2015

Ms. Helena Johannsen
Lingua Services
135 Maple Drive
Morningstar, WA 90807

Dear Ms. Johannsen:

I'm writing to inquire about your translation services and the possibility of a contract. As a professional filmmaker, I often need to hire translators to work on the translated subtitles of my films and materials. I understand that you offer an annual contract for services such as this in face-to-face interactions, and I was wondering whether you would be interested in contracting to help me on an ongoing basis.

Instructional films have been edited and produced by my company for training purposes in varied workplaces. The types of films we produce cover topics that range from safety training to customer service instruction. Additionally, we are sometimes hired to produce informational films for use in educational settings, such as community colleges and trade schools. Often, the businesses and institutions that contract with us request that we provide subtitles for the films, sometimes in multiple languages. Sometimes, printed materials or handouts to accompany the films are also requested.

As you might imagine, this adds a layer to the level of expertise we are required to employ. These types of requests have become so frequent that it is in our best interests to contract with a professional translating company on a continual basis, so we are interested in hiring Lingua Services. We would send you the finished films in English, and you would provide the translated subtitles in other languages. The most common requests we receive are for Spanish, French, Vietnamese, and Mandarin. However, we have received occasional requests for a much wider variety of languages, including Dutch, Swahili, and Hindi.

We have selected Lingua Services because of your impeccable reputation and body of work. This contract would require your assurance that the subtitles and translations you provide are grammatically and culturally correct, and that you have taken every precaution to make sure this is true. In exchange, we are prepared to offer you a generous contract and continuous work. The work would begin as soon as you are prepared to start.

Please contact me at 555–131–2468 at your earliest convenience to discuss the possibility of our partnership. I look forward to taking your call.

Yours faithfully,

Andrea Philips

Andrea Philips
Marketing Manager

After Reading

3. When you have finished reading, respond to the questions below in the space provided. Be prepared to discuss your answers with your classmates.

   a. **Organization:** What do you notice about the structure of the letter? How does it begin? How does it end? Why are the ideas in this letter placed in this order?

   b. **Audience:** To whom is the letter written? How do you know? What is the relationship between the letter writer and the audience?

   c. **Purpose**: Why did the writer write the letter? What examples from the text support your response?

Check Your Understanding

4. How would you describe the tone of this letter? Do you think Ms. Philips succeeds in making this offer sound tempting? Why or why not?

5. This letter is written in a business, or formal, context. Look at the sample text again, and circle or highlight examples of word choice that convey an appropriate tone for a business or formal letter.

ACTIVITY 2
Writing a Business Letter as a Class

WRITING PROMPT: Pretend that your class is a group of artists working on a large collage of photos entitled "Youth in America." The photos you plan to use in your collage will be taken by eighth-graders from all over the United States. With your class, write a formal letter to classes of eighth-graders in other schools, requesting that each class send you photos taken by them to be used in the collage. Make sure your letter meets the requirements listed in the learning targets for business and other formal letters. Be sure your letter:

- Communicates the purpose clearly
- Maintains a professional tone
- Demonstrates a business context
- Follows the prescribed format
- Uses appropriate conventions

Refer to the Scoring Guide for this writing task at the end of the workshop to help you understand where to focus your attention and efforts.

Prewriting

1. Imagine that your class has received the request described in the prompt. What questions do you have about this art collage and the photos you are requested to send? Brainstorm a list of things you'd like to know. After brainstorming individually, you will pair-share your ideas before sharing them with the whole class. Add to your list as you hear classmates' comments.

2. Working with your classmates and teacher, share questions and decide the answers. This information will help you draft the letter you will write. Generate a list of ways that you might make this idea sound inspiring to other eighth-graders. How might you motivate them to follow through with your request?

3. Copy the graphic organizer onto your own paper. With the class, discuss what will go into the three parts of your business letter. As you discuss the letter, add ideas and information to the graphic organizer.

Business Letter	Possible Content
Beginning	
Middle	
Ending	

4. Select the most important information from the graphic organizer, and create a class outline for your letter. Decide how best to explain your project and make your request. Keep in mind that part of your task is to present your collage idea in a way that is compelling and interesting to other eighth-graders. Consider your voice as the writer; avoid slang words, and be as direct and as clear as possible when writing so that your audience takes you seriously.

5. Make a copy of the outline to use as you draft your letter.

Drafting

6. The opening paragraph of your letter should express your general purpose for writing the letter, along with some background information on the subject. Write the opening paragraph in small groups, and create a personal copy of your own.

7. Refer to the graphic organizer as your write the paragraphs of the body of your letter, following your teacher's guidance through the drafting process.

8. As a class, add a closing paragraph to the class-constructed letter. Remember to create a sense of closure before the salutation, as well as suggest a plan of action for next steps in working with the audience to achieve your goal.

Check Your Understanding

After you have completed this process, read over the completed letter that your class has created. Refer to the Scoring Guide to help determine how well the letter meets the requirements. Consider the following:
• Underline the purpose of the letter. Are the purpose and audience clear?
• Circle the arguments/explanations used to support your purpose. Are these specific and appropriate?
• Is the language of the letter appropriate to eighth-graders? Is the language formal and without slang?
• Does the letter provide closure and suggest further action?

Revising for Language and Writer's Craft

When you write a sentence, you may choose between two *voices:* active and passive. In most sentences with an active verb, the subject performs the action indicated by the verb. This is called the active voice.

Conversely, in a sentence that employs the passive voice, the subject is being acted upon. The acting agent is not mentioned, or may be mentioned later. Study the following sentences taken from the sample text. Compare the active and passive voices.
• Active Voice: "The types of films we produce cover topics that range from safety training to customer service instruction."
• Active Voice: "Often, the businesses and institutions that contract with us request that we provide subtitles for the films, sometimes in multiple languages."

ACADEMIC VOCABULARY
In writing, the term voice may refer to:
• the author's writing style
• the person (first or third)
• the structure of a sentence (active or passive)

- Passive Voice: "Instructional films have been edited and produced by my company for training purposes in varied workplaces."
- Passive Voice: "Sometimes, printed materials or handouts to accompany the films are also requested."

9. For each of the sentences above, identify the verb(s) or verb phrase(s). Then, find the acting agent that executes these verbs. Notice that in each of the sentences that employ the active voice, the subject of the sentence is the acting agent. In the sentences that employ the passive voice, the acting agent is not the subject and may or may not be mentioned at all.

   Rewrite each of the passive sentences in the active voice.

   a.

   b.

10. Which version of each sentence do you think better expresses the thought? Why?

Most sentences employ the active voice because the acting agent is an important part of the information conveyed. When the passive voice is employed, it means that the acting agent is not as important as the other pieces of information in the sentence.

11. With a partner, discuss how the meaning or emphasis in the following sentences changes when the active voice is changed to the passive voice.

    a. The construction company finished the remodeling job on the school in eight months. The remodeling project at the high school was finished in eight months.

    b. The accountant made some serious calculation errors in the final report. The final accounting report contained some serious calculation errors.

    c. Lionel painted the porch a vibrant hue of green. The porch is painted a vibrant hue of green.

Often, the active voice is considered a better choice than the passive voice. Sometimes, however, a sentence in the passive voice does a better job communicating the intended information in the preferred manner. For example, in sentence set letter B, the accountant may prefer the construction that employs the passive voice because it draws attention away from the person who made the mistakes.

12. Reread your class-constructed letter. Find the sentences that employ the passive voice. In each case, is the passive voice an appropriate choice? Are there any sentences that would better achieve their purpose by changing them to the passive voice? Working with a partner, make revisions to change the voice of sentences in the class-constructed business letter in the places you think are appropriate. Prepare to share your revisions with the class.

Editing

13. Remember that the elements of a formal or business letter are
    - Sender's address
    - Date
    - Inside address
    - Salutation
    - Body
    - Closing
    - Signature

    With your class, add a heading, date, inside address, salutation, closing, and signature to your letter.

14. Edit your class-constructed letter for spelling, punctuation, grammar, and capitalization. Write a final, error-free draft to send to your audience. Make sure someone in your class adds a handwritten signature to represent your group.

ACTIVITY 3
Writing a Business Letter with Peers

WRITING PROMPT: Think of a service that you or you and a partner could offer to other members of your community or neighborhood. Write a letter that explains the service you are offering and details the benefits you could offer to your community. Your purpose will be to convince the recipients to hire you for these services.

Be sure to:
- Communicate the purpose clearly
- Maintain formal tone
- Include appropriate reasons and arguments
- Include the elements of a business letter
- Use appropriate conventions

Refer to the Scoring Guide for this writing task to help you understand where to focus your attention and efforts.

Prewriting/Drafting

1. With your writing group, copy the graphic organizer you used to write your class-constructed letter. Complete the graphic organizer as you plan your peer-constructed letter.

   a. Brainstorm a list of questions the recipient might ask about your project, and generate answers to include in your letter.
   b. Create a list of ways that you could make this idea sound enticing to the recipients.
   c. Decide which of these details to use, and outline the order in which to use them.
   d. Draft the letter based on the outline.
   e. Create a sense of closure in the last paragraph. Be sure to offer a suggestion for next steps in the process.
   f. Read the letter together, making revisions as necessary. Keep in mind your purpose and audience when considering the tone and level of formality. Review active and passive voice options in sentence construction.
   g. Add the elements of a formal or business letter.

Peer Review

2. Upon completing your letter, you will evaluate and provide feedback for another group's letter, based on criteria established in the learning targets and the Scoring Guide. Use the Revision Checklist below to guide your peer review. Prepare to share your thoughts with the authors of the letter.

Business Letter Revision Checklist	
Audience	Is the word choice appropriate for the audience?
	Is the tone formal and businesslike, with no slang words?
Purpose	Did the writers establish a clear purpose in the opening paragraph?
	Did the writers use active and passive voice appropriately?
Reasons/Support	Are the reasons included in the letter specific and connected directly to the purpose?
	Do the reasons make the letter more or less effective?
	What suggestions do you have for making the reasoning more persuasive to the audience?
Ending	Does the final paragraph provide a sense of closure to the letter? If not, what could be added, changed, or removed to improve the closing paragraph?
	Does the letter suggest a plan for moving forward in the partnership?
Elements of a Business Letter	Does the letter contain all of the elements of a business letter: sender's address, date, inside address, salutation, body, closing, and signature?

Revising/Editing

3. After sharing your feedback and receiving feedback from your peers, work with your group to revise your letter as necessary.

4. Edit the draft for mistakes in spelling, punctuation, grammar, and capitalization, and produce a final draft for submission to your teacher.

Independent Writing

WRITING PROMPT: Think of a household product, personal product, or food item that you enjoy. Are there any brands that you always purchase or that you are always happy to see in your home? Write a letter to the company, expressing your opinions about the quality of the product you enjoy. In the letter, explain your history with this product, why you are so satisfied, and request more product information and/or promotional items. This letter should meet the requirements listed in the Learning Targets and Scoring Guide for formal/business letters.

Review the writing steps from the peer-constructed letter to businesses and apply them to your individually constructed letter.

a. Brainstorm a list of anticipated questions and information to answer each.

b. Create a list of ways that you could make this idea sound enticing to the company.

c. Decide which of these details to use, and outline the order in which to use them.

d. Draft the letter based on the outline.

e. Create a sense of closure in the last paragraph, and be sure to offer a suggestion or make a request for next steps in the relationship.

f. Read the letter, making revisions as necessary. Keep in mind your purpose and audience when considering the tone and level of formality.

g. Add the elements of a formal or business letter, and edit for mistakes. Review active and passive voice options in sentence construction.

h. Produce a final, polished draft to submit to your teacher.

i. With the proper approval, mail your letter to the company.

SCORING GUIDE

Scoring Criteria	Exemplary	Proficient	Emerging	Incomplete
Ideas	The letter • develops ideas with directness and clarity using a formal tone • includes significant relevant reasons/arguments appropriate to the purpose	The letter • develops ideas using a formal tone • includes reasons appropriate to the purpose	The letter • conveys vague or incomplete ideas • presents limited, vague, or inappropriate information or reasoning	The letter • conveys confusing or incomplete ideas • lacks information or reasoning
Structure	The letter • uses organization of a business letter effectively for a specific purpose and audience • opens with a clear statement of purpose • provides a strong and compelling sense of closure	The letter • uses organization of a business letter appropriately • opens with a sense of purpose • provides a clear sense of closure	The letter • shows limited knowledge of the organization of a business letter • opens with a vague or limited statement of purpose • provides little or limited closure	The letter • lacks knowledge of the organization of a business letter • lacks a statement of purpose • provides insufficient closure
Use of Language	The letter • uses formal language skillfully and effectively • chooses precise words specific to the purpose and audience • includes few, if any, errors in grammar, spelling, punctuation, and capitalization	The letter • uses language appropriate for the audience and purpose • chooses words appropriate to the purpose and audience • includes minor errors in grammar, spelling, punctuation, and capitalization that do not interfere with the reader's understanding	The letter • uses informal language or language that shows little awareness of audience or purpose • uses vague or inappropriate word choices • includes errors in grammar, spelling, punctuation, and capitalization that interfere with the reader's understanding or are so numerous that they detract from the meaning	The letter • uses informal language or language that shows a lack of awareness of audience or purpose • uses poor word choices • includes errors in grammar, spelling, punctuation, and capitalization that interfere with the reader's understanding or are so numerous that they detract from the meaning

Grammar Handbook

Part 1: Grammar

Words, Word Groups, and Sentences

Words: Parts of Speech

Part of Speech	Function	Examples
Noun	names a person, place, thing, or idea	Taylor, mayor, ship, Missouri River, log, happiness
Pronoun	takes the place of a noun or other pronoun	I, you, she, us, they, himself, this, who, whom, that, which, each, none
Verb	expresses an action or state of being	go, be, startle, break, feel, do
Adjective	modifies a noun or pronoun	green, large, English, two
Adverb	modifies a verb, adjective, or other adverb	suddenly, awhile, yesterday, really
Preposition	relates one word to another word	in, on, to, above, before, with, between
Conjunction	joins words or word groups	and, or, but, so, either ... or, because
Interjection	expresses emotion	ow, whew, uh-oh, hooray

Word Groups: Phrases

A **phrase** is a word group that functions as a specific part of speech and does NOT contain both a subject and its verb.

Kind of Phrase	Description	Examples
noun phrase	functions as a noun (names a person, place, thing, or idea)	**The cold, dark woods** looked like **a forbidding place to be.**
verb phrase	functions as a verb (expresses an action or state of being)	We **were looking** for his house, where the old parrot cage **was stored**.
adjective phrase	functions as an adjective (modifies a noun or pronoun)	The book **on the left** is the one **to read** if you are working on the report **assigned in class.**
adverb phrase	functions as an adverb (modifies a verb, adjective, or other adverb)	He turned **to the left** when he was ready **to leave**.
participial phrase	begins with a past or present participle and functions as an adjective (modifies a noun or pronoun)	The book **sitting on the shelf** is the one **given by Uncle Dan**; you can use it for the report **assigned in class.**
infinitive phrase	begins with an infinitive verb form (to + base form) and functions as a noun, adjective, or adverb	He wants **to leave the theater** whenever you are ready **to go home**.
gerund phrase	begins with an –*ing* verb form and functions as a noun	**Leaving the theater early** and **going home** are our next steps.
prepositional phrase	introduced by a preposition and usually acts as an adjective or adverb	The book **on the left** is the one to read if you are working **on the report** assigned **in class.**

(continued)

appositive phrase	renames or identifies another noun or pronoun	My best friends, **Meredith and Emily**, say that they are going to New Orleans, **my favorite city**.
absolute phrase	consists of a noun and its modifiers and functions as a modifier of a verb or whole clause.	**The sunset waning**, we decided to head back to camp. There, we found our friend Jackson, **his backpack leaning against the picnic table**.

Word Groups: Clauses

A **clause** is a word group that contains both a subject and its verb. An **independent clause** can stand alone as a sentence and expresses a complete thought. A **dependent clause**, or **subordinate clause**, does not express a complete thought and cannot stand alone as a sentence.

Independent clause: **The pear tree grows.**
Dependent clause: The pear tree **that Aunt Kim gave us** grows well.

Dependent clauses can function as nouns, adjectives, or adverbs.

Noun clause: Do you know **who planted the tree**?
Adjective clause: Do you see the birds **that are nesting**?
Adverb clause: We'll start the mosaic **after Eric arrives**.

A **noun clause** functions as a noun does—for example, as the subject of a sentence or as a direct or indirect object.

Whoever wants a copy should send me a message.

An **adjective clause,** or **relative clause**, modifies a noun or pronoun. Adjective clauses can be **restrictive** (essential to a sentence's meaning) or **nonrestrictive** (nonessential to the sentence's meaning). Nonrestrictive clauses are set off by commas.

Restrictive: The boys **who want a copy** have added their names to the list.
Nonrestrictive: The four broken containers, **which are stacked in the corner**, need to be returned.

Sentences

A **sentence** is a word group that has both a subject and a verb and that expresses a complete thought. Sentences are made of words, phrases, and clauses. A **phrase** is a word group that functions as a specific part of speech and does NOT contain both a subject and its verb. A **clause** is a word group that contains both a subject and its verb and that may act as a part of speech.

A **simple sentence** is made of one independent clause and no dependent clauses. It may contain any number of phrases.

The pear tree grows.
The pear tree given to us by Aunt Kim grows very well in that corner of the yard.

A **compound sentence** is made of two or more independent clauses and no dependent clauses. It may contain any number of phrases.

The sun shines, and the pear tree grows.
The pear tree given to us by Aunt Kim grows very well in that corner of the yard, and we may plant another one near it in the fall.

A **complex sentence** is made of one independent clause and at least one dependent clause. It may contain any number of phrases.

The pear tree that we planted last season grows well.
The pear tree that we planted last season and that Aunt Kim gave us grows well.

A **compound-complex sentence** is made of one independent clause and at least one dependent clause. It may contain any number of phrases.

The pear tree that we planted last season grows well, and so does the apple tree.
The pear tree that we planted last season and that Aunt Kim gave us grows well, and so does the apple tree.

Part 2: Usage

Subject-Verb Agreement

Compound Subjects

When the subject of a sentence is composed of two or more nouns or pronouns connected by *and*, use a plural verb.

Sara and **her sisters are** at the movie theater.

When two or more singular nouns or pronouns are connected by *or* or *nor*, use a singular verb.

Clive or **Penny is** in the yard.

When a compound subject contains both a singular and a plural noun or pronoun joined by *or* or *nor*, the verb should agree with the noun or pronoun that is nearer the verb.

George or **his teammates practice** daily.

Other Problems in Agreement

Doesn't is a contraction of *does not* and should be used with a singular subject. *Don't* is a contraction of *do not* and should be used with a plural subject. Exception: With the pronouns *I* and *you*, the contraction *don't* should be used.

He doesn't **like** it.
They don't **like** it.

Do not be misled by a phrase that comes between the subject and the verb. The verb agrees with the subject, not with a noun or pronoun in the interrupting phrase.

One of the stores **is** closed.
The people who love that band **are** many.
The captain of the team, as well as his rivals, **is** ready.
The movie, including all the trailers that come before, **is** very long.
A teenager with a skateboard and basketball **walks** past this bus stop each day.

The terms *each, each one, either, neither, everyone, everybody, anybody, anyone, nobody, somebody, someone,* and *no one* are singular and require a singular verb.

Each of these platters **is** full.
Everybody knows the answer.
Either is fine with me.

Some nouns that are plural in form, such as *civics*, *mathematics*, *measles*, and *news*, require singular verbs.

Measles is a serious illness.

Some nouns, such as *scissors*, *tweezers*, *pants*, and *shears*, identify singular objects but name things that have two parts. These nouns take plural verbs.

These **scissors are** sharp.
Those **pants are** made of heavy fabric.

In sentences beginning with *there is* or *there are*, the subject follows the verb, but the verb must still agree with the subject.

There **are** many **owls** in the woods.
There **is** a **question**.

Collective nouns are words that can take a singular or plural verb, depending on if they refer to the group as a whole or to the group as a collection of different members or elements. Examples include *group*, *team*, *committee*, *class*, and *family*.

The **family has** a long history.
My **family have** never been able to agree.

Pronoun-Antecedent Agreement

When a pronoun takes the place of a singular noun, use a singular pronoun.

Incorrect: If a student parks a car on campus, they have to buy a parking sticker.
Correct: If a **student** parks a car on campus, **he or she** has to buy a parking sticker.

If using *he or she* sounds wordy, you can revise a sentence to use a plural form instead:

Students who park on campus have to buy parking stickers for **their** cars.

The pronouns *each*, *each one*, *either*, *neither*, *everyone*, *everybody*, *anybody*, *anyone*, *nobody*, *somebody*, *someone*, and *no one* require a singular verb.

Everybody ought to do **his or her** job.
Neither of the girls brought **her** backpack.

Other Problems in Agreement

Agreement in Person

Pronouns should agree in person with their antecedents. Do not switch between first, second, and third person without reason.

Incorrect: When a person comes to class, you should have your homework ready.
Correct: A **person** arriving in class should have **his or her** homework ready.

Clear Reference

Pronouns should refer specifically and clearly to their antecedents. In some cases, you may need to reword or reorganize a sentence to make it clearer.

Ambiguous: Although the car hit the building, it was not damaged. [Is *it* the car or the building?]
Revised: Although it hit the building, the car was not damaged.
Ambiguous: Stella told Kathryn that she ought to help build the set. [Does *she* refer to Stella or Kathryn?]
Revised: According to Stella, Kathryn ought to help build the set.

Unclear: In the newspaper they say that the drought will last all summer. [Who are "they"?]
Revised: An article in the newspaper says that the drought will last all summer.
Unclear: Armand had a job as a ranger in a state forest last summer. This may be his life's work. [What word does this refer to?]
Revised: Armand had a job as a ranger in a state forest last summer. Protecting nature may be his life's work.

Pronoun Case

Pronouns have three cases.

- **Subjective (nominative) case:** pronouns used as subjects or predicate nominatives
- **Objective case:** pronouns used as objects of verbs or prepositions
- **Possessive case:** pronouns that express ownership

Subjective Case	Objective Case	Possessive Case
I	me	my (mine)
you	you	your (yours)
he, she, it	him, her, it	his, her (hers), it (its)
we	us	our (ours)
they	them	their (theirs)
who	whom	whose

Reflexive and Intensive Pronouns

	Singular	Plural
First person	myself	ourselves
Second person	yourself	yourselves
Third person	himself, herself, itself	themselves

A **reflexive pronoun** refers back to the subject of a clause or sentence. It functions as a complement or as the object of a preposition.

I told myself to be brave. [The reflexive pronoun is the indirect object of *told*.]

An **intensive pronoun** emphasizes the word it refers to.

I myself led the team to safety. [The reflexive pronoun emphasizes the subject.]

Compound Structures

In compound structures that include two pronouns or a noun and a pronoun, pay attention to pronoun case. Hint: If you're not sure which form to use, try each pronoun on its own in the sentence.

Incorrect: Dylan and me play soccer. [Would you say, "me play"?]
Correct: Dylan and I play soccer.

Incorrect: He gave the message to the faculty and I. [Would you say, "he gave the message to I"?]
Correct: He gave the message to the faculty and me.

Incorrect: Us musicians like the conductor. [Would you say, "us like the conductor"?]
Correct: We musicians like the conductor.

Comparisons

In comparisons, pay attention to pronoun case. Hint: You can finish the comparison, as shown below, to determine which case to use.

> Connor is more talented **than I** (am).
> This helps Eliot **as much as** (it helps) **me**.

Who and *Whom*

In formal writing, use *whom* and its related forms as an object of a verb or of a preposition.

> **Informal:** Who am I talking to?
> **Formal:** To **whom** am I talking?
> **Informal:** I will be sitting next to whoever Senator Gorm invites.
> **Formal:** I will be sitting next to **whomever** Senator Gorm invites.

Appositives

An **appositive** is a noun or pronoun that identifies or explains another noun or pronoun.

> Your friend **Bill** is in Dr. Levine's AP class.
> My sister's cat, **Chimmy**, doesn't like your dog.

An **appositive phrase** usually follows the word it explains or identifies, but it may also precede it.

> **A state known for its cold climate**, Alaska is closer to the North Pole than to Texas.

Some appositives are **restrictive**, or essential to a sentence's meaning. Restrictive appositives are not set off by punctuation.

> The civil rights leader **Martin Luther King, Jr.** is often quoted. [Without the appositive, we would not know who is often quoted.]

If the appositive is **nonrestrictive**, or not essential to a sentence's meaning, it is set off with commas.

> Martin Luther King, Jr. **a famous civil rights leader**, is often quoted. [Without the appositive, we would still know who is often quoted.]

Verbals

Gerunds and Gerund Phrases

A **gerund** is a verbal that ends in *–ing* and functions as a noun. Since a gerund functions as a noun, it can be used as a subject, direct object, subject complement, or object of preposition.

> **Traveling** might satisfy your desire for new experiences.
> Are you excited about **arriving**?

Gerund phrases include a gerund and any modifiers or complements of the gerund. A gerund phrase functions as a noun.

> **Traveling to Asia** might satisfy your desire for new experiences.
> Are you excited about **arriving tomorrow**?

Participles and Participial Phrases

A **participle** is a verbal that is used as an adjective and most often ends in *–ing* or *–ed*. Participles modify nouns or pronouns. Present participles end in *–ing*. Past participles end in *–ed, –d, –en, –t,* or *–n*, as in the words *used, beaten, dealt,* and *seen*.

The **dangling** toy caught the kitten's attention.
The **broken** shutter banged in the wind.

A **participial phrase** includes the participle and any modifiers or complements of the participle. A participial phrase modifies a noun or pronoun.

The toy **dangling off the sofa** caught the kitten's attention.
The shutter **broken in the winter storm** banged in the wind.

A participial phrase should clearly modify a word in the sentence and should be placed near the word it modifies.

Incorrect: Carrying a stack of plates, his foot caught on a step. [His foot was not carrying plates. This participial phrase is a **dangling modifier**; it does not clearly modify any word in the sentence.]
Correct: Carrying a stack of plates, he caught his foot on a step.
Incorrect: Flying across the sky, Eugene saw a huge flock of gorgeous birds. [Eugene was not flying. This participial phrase is a **misplaced modifier**; it appears to modify *Eugene* rather than *flock*.]
Correct: Eugene saw a huge flock of gorgeous birds **flying across the sky.**

Punctuating Participial Phrases

When a participial phrase begins a sentence, a comma should be placed after the phrase.

Arriving at the park, Tara found that it had just closed.
Exercising regularly, Miguel found that his health and his attitude both improved.

When a participial phrase comes in the middle of a sentence, it should be set off with commas only if the information in the phrase is not essential to the meaning of the sentence.

Gricelda, **performing in the play**, found that she enjoyed being onstage. [not essential]
The teenager **performing in the play** was very talented. [essential]

When a participial phrase comes at the end of a sentence, a comma usually precedes the phrase if it modifies an earlier word in the sentence but not if the phrase directly follows the word it modifies.

The rangers watched the caribou **heading toward the stream**. [The phrase modifies *caribou*.]
The rangers watched the caribou, **admiring the animals' beauty and strength**. [The phrase modifies *rangers*, not *caribou*.]

Infinitives and Infinitive Phrases

An infinitive is a verbal consisting of the word *to* and the base form of a verb. It can function as a noun, adjective, or adverb. The infinitive may function as a subject, direct object, subject complement, adjective, or adverb in a sentence.

To stay seemed rude. [subject]
Jerome wanted **to go**. [direct object]
Her preference was **to delay**. [predicate nominative]
He lacked the willingness **to insist**. [adjective]
They finally were ready **to depart**. [adverb]

Don't confuse an infinitive—a verbal consisting of *to* plus a verb—with a prepositional phrase beginning with *to*.

Infinitives: to paint, to become, to exit, to sit, to throw
Prepositional phrases: to Jason, to the field, to all of us, to the hour

An **infinitive phrase** includes an infinitive and its modifiers or complements.

> **To stay past 10:00 p.m.** seemed rude. [subject]
> Jerome wanted **to go right away.** [direct object]
> Her preference was **to delay till her aunt arrived**. [predicate nominative]
> He lacked the willingness **to insist that they say good night**. [adjective]
> They finally were ready **to depart around midnight**. [adverb]

Punctuating Infinitives and Infinitive Phrases

If an infinitive or infinitive phrase is used as an adverb and begins a sentence, it should be set off with a comma; otherwise, no punctuation is needed.

> **To convince me to read the book**, Jacob read me his favorite passages. [adverb]
> **To plant a garden** is my next goal. [noun]

Split Infinitives

Split infinitives occur when words come between *to* and the verb in an infinitive. Although splitting infinitives is sometimes acceptable, it is often awkward, and some readers find split infinitives overly informal. You may wish to avoid splitting infinitives in formal writing.

> **Awkward:** He began **to**, all of a sudden, **talk** excitedly about his new job.
> **Revised:** He began, all of a sudden, **to talk** excitedly about his new job.

Prepositions

Preposition Use: Expressions of Time

On is used with days:

> I will see Tim on Wednesday.

At is used with *noon, night, midnight,* and with the time of day:

> The movie is **at** noon.

In is used with other parts of the day, with months, with years, with seasons:

> We will gather **in** the afternoon.
> **In** the spring, we can visit Kansas.

To express continuing action, English uses the following prepositions: *since, for, by, from ... to, from ... until, during, (with)in.*

> The visitors have been here **since** yesterday.
> I'm going to Atlanta **for** two weeks.
> Mike's cousins were in Austin **from** August **to** October.

Preposition Use: Expressions of Place

English uses the following prepositions:

- to talk about a specific point or place: *in*
  There is an egg **in** the nest.
- to express something contained: *inside*
  What is **inside** that blue box?
- to talk about the surface: *on*
  What is **on** the counter?
- to talk about a general vicinity: *at*
  We left him **at** Antietam.

Preposition Use: Objects of Verbs

English uses the following prepositions to introduce objects of the following verbs.

At: *glance, laugh, look, rejoice, smile, stare*

> I'm laughing **at** the puppets' antics.
> The toddler smiled **at** you.

Of: *approve, consist, smell*

> Aunt Irene approves **of** your career choice.
> That smells **of** mildew.

Of (or about): *dream, think*

> Zac dreams **of** starting anew.
> Zeb thinks **about** leaving for Seattle.

For: *call, hope, look, wait, watch, wish*

> Caroline hopes **for** success.
> The stranded sailor waits and watches **for** rescue.

Sentence Construction: Connecting Clauses

Coordinating conjunctions and **conjunctive adverbs** can be used to connect independent clauses.

Coordinating Conjunctions: The coordinating conjunctions used to join independent clauses are *and, but, or, for, nor, so,* and *yet.* When the second independent clause in a sentence begins with a coordinating conjunction, a comma is needed before the coordinating conjunction:

> Ben wanted to play soccer, **but** Miles wanted to run track.

Conjunctive Adverbs: Some common conjunctive adverbs are *also, consequently, furthermore, however, moreover, nevertheless,* and *therefore.* A conjunctive adverb can begin an independent clause or can be used to join independent clauses. When the second independent clause in a sentence has a conjunctive adverb, a semicolon is needed before it.

> Ben wanted to play soccer; **however**, Miles wanted to run track.

Subordinating conjunctions can connect dependent clauses to independent clauses. Common subordinating conjunctions include *after, although, as, as if, because, before, even if, even though, if, in order to, since, though, unless, until, when, whenever, whether,* and *while.*

> **Even if** she does prefer vanilla, I think she will enjoy the coconut cake.
> I will help you with the dishes **whenever** you are ready.
> The chicken likes to roost outside **unless** it is raining.

Common Sentence Construction Errors

Comma Splices: A comma splice is the use of a comma to join two independent clauses. You can usually fix the error in one of these ways:

- changing the comma to a period and turning the two clauses into separate sentences
- changing the comma to a semicolon
- making one clause dependent by inserting a subordinating conjunction
- adding a coordinating conjunction after the comma

Incorrect:
I love that movie, I have watched it 10 times.
Correct:
I love that movie. I have watched it 10 times.
I love that movie; I have watched it 10 times.
Because I love that movie, I have watched it 10 times.
I love that movie, and I have watched it 10 times.

Fused Sentences: A fused sentence is two or more independent clauses run together with no punctuation. This error is also known as a run-on sentence. The error can sometimes be corrected by adding a period, semicolon, or colon between the clauses.

Incorrect: I love that movie I have watched it 10 times.
Correct: I love that movie. I have watched it 10 times.
Correct: I love that movie; I have watched it 10 times.
Correct: I love that movie: I have watched it 10 times.

Sentence Fragments: A sentence fragment is a word group that does not express a complete thought and cannot stand alone as a sentence. You can usually fix a fragment by combining it with another sentence to make a complete thought or by removing a subordinating conjunction.

Incorrect: Because today I have band practice.
Correct: Because today I have band practice, I won't be riding the bus.
Correct: Today I have band practice.

Using Verbs Correctly

Verbs express different times through tenses. Do not change tenses unnecessarily. Use tenses consistently unless you are deliberately expressing differences in time or sequence.

Inconsistent: I **was talking** to Roseanne, and I **say**, "Will you be in Florida in June?"
Consistent: I **was talking** to Roseanne, and I **said**, "Will you be in Florida in June?"

Sequence of Tenses
Present Perfect: They have walked.
Present: They walk.
Past Perfect: They had walked.
Past: They walked.
Future Perfect: They will have walked.
Future: They will walk.

Problems in sequencing tenses usually occur with the perfect tenses, which are formed by adding an auxiliary or auxiliaries to the past participle.

Verb	Past Form	Perfect Tenses
ring	rang	has/have/had rung; will have rung
walk	walked	has/have/had walked; will have walked

The most common auxiliaries are *can, do, may, must, ought, shall, will, has, have, had,* and forms of *be.*

Present Perfect: The present perfect consists of a past participle preceded by has or have. It expresses action that began in the past and that continues into the present.

Past: Ms. Gage **taught** for 10 years. [She no longer teaches.]
Present Perfect: Ms. Gage **has taught** for 10 years. [She is still teaching.]

Past Perfect: The past perfect tense expresses action in the past that is completed before another past action.

Past: Mr. Geiser played in a band for years.
Past Perfect: Mr. Geiser had played in a band for years before he went solo.

Future Perfect: The future perfect tense expresses action that will have been completed at a specified time in the future.

Future: Mr. Catalano will teach for 17 years.
Future Perfect: Mr. Catalano will have taught for 17 years this November.

Mood and Modal Forms

Mood refers to the form the verb takes to indicate the speaker's attitude. Avoid unnecessary shifts in mood.

Indicative mood expresses a fact or opinion. It is used in declarative sentences.

The Rogers family **raises** chickens.

Imperative mood expresses a command or request.

Bring me the eggs, please.

Subjunctive mood expresses a suggestion, necessity, condition contrary to fact, or a wish.

I recommend that you **be seated** now.
It is necessary that you **be seated**.
If I **were** you, I would be seated.
I wish I **were** seated already.

Interrogative sentences express a question.

Did you **go** to the farm?
Are they **raising** chickens?

Conditional verbs express actions or states of being that depend on other conditions.

If the sun had already set, we **would have gone** home.

Irregular Verbs

In English, verbs have a base form (the present), a past form, and a past participle. Regular verbs add *–ed* to the base form to make both the past form and past participle. Irregular verbs do not follow this pattern.

Present	Past	Past Participle
be	was, were	been
become	became	become
begin	began	begun
blow	blew	blown
break	broke	broken
bring	brought	brought
build	built	built

(continued)

burst	burst	burst
buy	bought	bought
catch	caught	caught
choose	chose	chosen
come	came	come
cut	cut	cut
deal	dealt	dealt
do	did	done
drink	drank	drunk
drive	drove	driven
eat	ate	eaten
fall	fell	fallen
feed	fed	fed
feel	felt	felt
fight	fought	fought
find	found	found
fly	flew	flown
forbid	forbade	forbidden
forget	forgot	forgotten
forgive	forgave	forgiven
freeze	froze	frozen
get	got	gotten
give	gave	given
go	went	gone
grow	grew	grown
have	had	had
hear	heard	heard
hide	hid	hidden
hold	held	held
hurt	hurt	hurt
keep	kept	kept
know	knew	known
lay	laid	laid
lead	led	led
leave	left	left
let	let	let
lie	lay	lain
lose	lost	lost
make	made	made
meet	met	met
pay	paid	paid

quit	quit	quit
read	read	read
ride	rode	ridden
run	ran	run
say	said	said
see	saw	seen
seek	sought	sought
sell	sold	sold
send	sent	sent
shake	shook	shaken
shine	shone	shone
sing	sang	sung
sit	sat	sat
sleep	slept	slept
speak	spoke	spoken
spend	spent	spent
spring	sprang	sprung
stand	stood	stood
steal	stole	stolen
swim	swam	swum
swing	swung	swung
take	took	taken
teach	taught	taught
tear	tore	torn
tell	told	told
think	thought	thought
throw	threw	thrown
understand	understood	understood
wake	woke (waked)	woken (waked)
wear	wore	worn
win	won	won
write	wrote	written

Commonly Confused Verbs

Lie vs. Lay		
Present	**Past**	**Past Participle**
lie, lying (to tell a falsehood)	I lied to no one.	I have lied to no one.
lie, lying (to recline)	I lay in bed because I was tired.	He has lain in bed all morning.
lay, laying (to put, place)	I laid the doll in the cradle.	We have laid the doll in the cradle.

Sit vs. Set		
Present	**Past**	**Past Participle**
sit (to be seated or come to a resting position)	I sat on the curb to wait.	You have sat on the curb all afternoon.
set (to put or place)	I set my dish in the sink.	She has set her dishes in the sink.

Rise vs. Raise		
Present	**Past**	**Past Participle**
rise (steady or customary upward movement)	The helicopter rose into the air.	The helicopter has risen into the air.
raise (to cause to rise)	They raised their hands to give the answer.	I have raised my hands in class many times.

Part 3: Style

Parallel Structure

Parallel structure is the use of similar grammatical structures to show that two or more ideas are similar in importance or meaning or to provide emphasis. Words, phrases, and clauses can be parallel.

Words and Phrases

Not Parallel: Carla likes hik**ing**, swimm**ing**, and **to ride** a bicycle.
Parallel: Carla likes hik**ing**, swimm**ing**, and rid**ing** a bicycle.

Not Parallel: The manager wrote his report quick**ly**, accurate**ly**, and **in a detailed manner**.
Parallel: The manager wrote his report quick**ly**, accurate**ly**, and thorough**ly**.

Not Parallel: He wait**ed** until the last minute to study for the exam, completed his lab problems in a careless manner, and **his motivation was** low.
Parallel: He wait**ed** until the last minute to study for the exam, complet**ed** his lab problems in a careless manner, and lack**ed** motivation.

Clauses

Not Parallel: The teacher told the students **that they should get** a lot of sleep, **that they should not worry** too much, and **to go over their notes**.
Parallel: The teacher told the students **that they should get** a lot of sleep, **that they should not worry** too much, and **that they should go over their notes**.

Not Parallel: I asked **when the order would be ready, where the package should be delivered**, and **the name of the recipient**.
Parallel: I asked **when the order would be ready, where the package should be delivered**, and **who would receive the package**.

Lists

Be sure to keep the elements in a list parallel.

> **Not Parallel:** The tutorial covers how to **identify clauses**, **correct common errors**, and **proofreading for errors**.

Parallel: The tutorial covers how to **identify clauses**, **correct common errors**, and **proofread for errors**.

Bulleted items should be parallel.

Not Parallel:

The master gardener talked about these topics:

- compost
- wildflowers
- eradicating pests
- irrigation

Parallel:

The master gardener talked about these topics:

- compost
- wildflowers
- pests
- irrigation

Using Active Voice

In a sentence using **active voice**, the subject of the sentence performs the action expressed by the verb.

The girl **threw** the ball.
I **ate** three apples yesterday.

In a sentence using **passive voice**, the subject of the sentence receives the action expressed by the verb.

The ball **was thrown**.
Three apples **were eaten** yesterday.

	Active	Passive
Simple Present	Acme **ships** the widgets to many clients.	Widgets **are shipped** to many clients.
Present Progressive	The chef **is cooking** the beets.	The beets **are being cooked**.
Simple Past	I **mailed** a letter last Friday.	A letter **was mailed** last Friday.
Past Progressive	The principal **was making** announcements at the assembly.	Announcements **were being made** at the assembly.
Future	The president **will make** decisions.	Decisions **will be made** by the president.
Present Perfect	Kelli **has made** the appointment.	The appointment **has been made**.
Past Perfect	They **had baked** muffins for us.	Muffins **had been baked** for us.
Future Perfect	By Tuesday, we **will have completed** this project.	By Tuesday, this project **will have been completed**.

The active voice is more vigorous and direct. There are times when passive voice is useful or appropriate—for instance, when you want to be diplomatic and avoid naming names, or when you want to emphasize the recipient of the action. However, generally, you should use active voice most of the time. Avoid unnecessary shifts in voice.

Part 4: Mechanics

Capitalization

Capitalize the first word of a sentence.

> Do you have my schedule?

Capitalize the pronoun *I*.

> When I sneeze, I try not to do so loudly.

Capitalize proper nouns (the names of specific people, places, organizations, and things).

Dreiser Company	Brooklyn Bridge
Supreme Court	Cleveland, Ohio
Indian Ocean	Federal Trade Commission

Capitalize proper names of family members.

> I sent cookies to Grandma but not to Uncle Joe.
> What did Father say?

Lowercase words for family members when they are preceded by *a*, *an*, *the*, or a possessive pronoun.

> Carina is an aunt now.
> I sent cookies to our grandmothers but not our uncles.
> What did your father say?

Capitalize the names of specific deities, religious figures, and holy books.

God	Abraham
the Virgin Mary	Shiva
the Bible	Buddha
Mercury	Zeus
the Torah	the Koran

Exception: Do not capitalize the nonspecific use of the word *god*.

> The Greek gods seem almost human at times.

Capitalize titles preceding names but not titles that follow names.

> What do you think of Mayor Nagin?
> I voted for Cecilia Guerra, the mayor of Nettontown.

Capitalize directions that are used as names of parts of the country.

> The Rogers family has lived in the South for several generations.

Note: Do not capitalize directions when they are not used as names.

> We are heading south next week.

Capitalize days of the week, months of the year, and holidays.

Easter	Monday
January	September
Friday	Thanksgiving

Capitalize the names of seasons only when they are part of a proper noun.

Brentwood Fall Festival
2016 Summer Olympics

Capitalize the names of countries, nationalities, and specific languages.

Paraguay   Russia
Spanish   Russian

Capitalize the first word in a sentence that is a direct quotation.

George Saunders said, "Grief is the bill that comes due for love."

Capitalize the first, last, and all important words in titles of literary and artistic works.
Do not capitalize short prepositions or the articles *a*, *an*, and *the* unless used as the first word of the title.

The Catcher in the Rye
"Nothing Gold Can Stay"
Starry Night

Capitalize the names of members of national, political, racial, social, civic, and athletic groups.

New Orleans Saints   Republicans
African Americans   Phi Beta Kappa
Golden State Warriors   Japanese

Capitalize historical periods and major events.

Edwardian Era   Boston Tea Party
Great Depression   Louisiana World Exposition

Note: Do not capitalize names of centuries.

sixteenth century
first century

Capitalize trademarked brand names.

Pepsi   IBM
Toyota   Nintendo

Punctuating Sentences
Here are basic sentence patterns and how they are punctuated.

Simple Sentence
This pattern is an example of a simple sentence.

Independent clause [.]
We went on an urban hike downtown.

Compound Sentence with a Comma and Coordinating Conjunction

This pattern is an example of a compound sentence with a coordinating conjunction.

Independent clause [,] **coordinating conjunction** *independent clause* [.]

These are the coordinating conjunctions: *and, but, for, or, nor, so, yet.* Note that *then* is not a coordinating conjunction and cannot be used with a comma to separate independent clauses.

We went on an urban hike downtown, and we took notes on the world around us.

Compound Sentence with a Semicolon

This pattern is an example of a compound sentence with a semicolon.

Independent clause [;] *independent clause* [.]

We went on an urban hike downtown; we took notes on the world around us.

Compound Sentence with a Conjunctive Adverb

This pattern is an example of a compound sentence with a conjunctive adverb.

Independent clause [;] **conjunctive adverb** [,] *independent clause* [.]

These are examples of conjunctive adverbs: *also, consequently, however, moreover, therefore, thus.*

We went on an urban hike downtown; also, we took notes on the world around us.

Complex Sentence Beginning with a Dependent Clause

This pattern is an example of a complex sentence. It begins with a subordinating conjunction and a subordinate (dependent) clause.

Subordinating conjunction *dependent clause* [,] *independent clause* [.]

These are examples of subordinating conjunctions: *after, although, as, as if, because, before, if, since, until, when, while.*

When we went on an urban hike downtown, we took notes on the world around us.

Complex Sentence Beginning with an Independent Clause

This pattern is an example of a complex sentence beginning with an independent clause.

Independent clause **subordinating conjunction** *dependent clause* [.]
We took notes on the world around us while we were on an urban hike downtown.

Independent Clause with an Embedded Nonessential Phrase or Clause

This pattern includes an independent clause with an embedded nonessential clause or phrase. A nonessential clause or phrase can be removed without changing the basic meaning of the sentence or making it ungrammatical. The nonessential clause or phrase provides extra information, but the sentence can stand alone without it.

First part of independent clause [,] **nonessential clause or phrase** [,] *rest of the independent clause* [.]
We took notes, some serious and some humorous, on the world around us.
We took notes, which we used later in reports, on the world around us.

Independent Clause with an Embedded Essential Phrase or Clause

This pattern includes an independent clause with an embedded essential clause or phrase. An essential clause or phrase cannot be removed without changing the basic meaning of the sentence.

> *First part of an independent clause* **essential clause or phrase** *rest of the independent clause* [.]
> The next hike that we will take will go along Main Street.
> The next hike through downtown will go along Main Street.

Commas

Commas are often used between grammatical elements and have many conventional uses. Here are essential rules for comma use.

Use a comma with a coordinating conjunction **to join two independent clauses** (*and, but, or, for, nor, so, yet*).

> Rain fell last weekend, but this weekend should be sunny.

Use a comma after an **introductory verbal phrase or an introductory adverb clause.**

> To see the meteors, you should go where there is less light pollution.
> Watching the meteors, we felt both excited and sleepy.
> Before we left, we packed extra snacks.

Use a comma after a long **introductory prepositional phrase** or after more than one prepositional phrase.

> By one o'clock in the morning, we were getting cold.

Use a comma after one short **introductory prepositional phrase** if needed for clarity or readability.

> In December, 17 meteors streaked above me as I watched. [Without the comma, it looks at first as if the sentence contains the date *December 17.*]

Use a comma to separate **items in a series**. For logic and consistency, it is helpful to include a final comma (called the serial comma, or Oxford comma) before the conjunction; however, it is usually not incorrect to omit it.

> The trail was long, dusty, and arduous.
> I like to read novels by George Eliot, Charles Dickens, and E. M. Forster.
> They invited my parents, Frank, and Peggy. [Note that without the serial comma, it would be unclear whether two or four people were invited.]

Use a comma to set off **nonessential phrases and clauses**.

> My hen, a Rhode Island Red, lays several eggs each week.
> Russell Hoban's novel *Riddley Walker*, which I am reading, is fascinating.

Use a comma between **coordinate adjectives** (adjectives that have equal weight and that can be reordered in the sentence).

> He turned in a concise, well-written essay.

If you cannot change the order of the adjectives without making the sentence sound awkward or unidiomatic, you may not need commas.

> His skateboard is the big green one. [You wouldn't say "green big one."]
> The routine involves an easy high kick. [You wouldn't say "high easy kick."]

Use a comma after a **transitional word or phrase**, such as *however, therefore, nonetheless, also, otherwise, finally, instead, thus, of course, above all, for example, in other words, as a result, on the other hand, in conclusion, in addition*.

> Nonetheless, we will proceed as planned.
> Otherwise, we will be stranded here without our phones.

Use a comma to set off **direct quotations and speech tags**.

> "Hey," Roy said, "I will be taking photos at the gallery reception."
> Emily replied, "I hope you get good pictures of Katherine and Alan."

Use commas to set off **items in a date**.

> She was born on October 27, 1962.
> That was due on Friday, April 12, 2013, but was turned in late.

Use commas to set off **thousands, millions, billions**, and so on.

> 27,000,000

Use commas to set off **personal titles and suffixes**. Note that in running text, a comma follows the title or suffix.

> Please welcome Michael Davidson, M.D., to the stage.
> The next speaker was Monica Sanchez, attorney at law, who once attended our school.

Use a comma to separate a **city name** from a state or country name. In running text, a comma follows the state or country name.

> I am from Salisbury, England, and she is from Edinburgh, Scotland.
> I ordered copies from a bookstore in Philadelphia, Pennsylvania, but they haven't arrived.

Semicolons

Use a semicolon to **join two independent clauses** when the second clause restates the first or when the two clauses are closely related.

> If you can arrive early, I will appreciate it; we'll have to set up the sound system.

Use a semicolon to join two independent clauses when the second clause begins with a conjunctive adverb, such as *however, therefore, moreover, furthermore, thus, meanwhile, nonetheless,* or *otherwise,* or a transition, such as *in fact, for example, that is, for instance, in addition, in other words, on the other hand,* or *even so*.

> The technician has already left; however, I think I have her cell number.

Use a semicolon to join items in a series when the items themselves include commas.

> My favorite cities are London, England; Dublin, Ireland; and Chicago, Illinois.

Colons

Use a colon to join two independent clauses when you want to emphasize the second clause.

> I'll ask you again: Would you please return the shirt you borrowed?

Use a colon after an independent clause when it introduces a list, a quotation, an appositive, or other idea directly related to the independent clause.

We need supplies for the party: ice, beverages, cups, and snacks.
This is Nelson's favorite quotation by George Eliot: "What do we live for, if it is not to make life less difficult for each other?"
Tasha has an idea for the perfect classroom pet: a turtle.

Use a colon after the greeting of a business letter.

To Whom It May Concern:

Use a colon to separate hours and minutes.

12:00 p.m.

Use a colon to separate the chapter and verse in a biblical reference.

1 John 4:7

Parentheses

Parentheses are used to set off explanatory content, especially if it is tangential.
Use parentheses to set off nonessential, or nonrestrictive, information such as dates, clarifying information, or sources, from a sentence.

David Foster Wallace (1962–2008) wrote both fiction and nonfiction.
You can find us at 1802 Quentin Street (just behind Compson Middle School).

Use parentheses to enclose literary citations or explanations of acronyms.

The Wired Northwest (Hirt, 2012) details the electrification of the Northwest.
The scientists at NIH (National Institutes of Health) will issue a report.

Brackets

Brackets are used to clarify the meaning of quoted material.

The biologist explained, "We were dismayed to find that it [the mantis shrimp] was capable of breaking the glass of the aquarium."
Dr. Carlisle replied, "The reform bill of the [eighteen-]thirties was in some ways problematic."

Quotation Marks

Use quotation marks to enclose direct quotations. Note that commas and periods are placed inside closing quotation marks, while colons and semicolons are placed outside. The placement of question and exclamation marks depends on meaning.

Monique asked, "What time does the plane land?" and Jay replied, "Right at noon."
Monique said, "I'll bring the car"; Jay replied, "Great!"
Did Jay really say, "I'm sure the plane will be late"?

Use quotation marks to indicate that a word is jargon, slang, or a new word, or is used ironically.

That's what is known as a "culture capture."
She raised an eyebrow at this "fair" decision but did not object.

Use quotation marks around the titles of short poems, songs, short stories, magazine or newspaper articles, essays, speeches, chapters, short films, and episodes of television or radio programs.

"Nothing Gold Can Stay," by Robert Frost
"Dizzy," by Tommy Roe
"City Council to Reconsider Redevelopment Plan," an article in the newspaper

Italics

Italicize the titles of magazines, books, newspapers, films, television programs, long poems, plays, operas, music albums, works of art, and individual spacecraft, trains, planes, or ships.

> *TIME*
> *Julius Caesar* by William Shakespeare
> *Starry Night* by Vincent van Gogh
> *Enterprise* (space shuttle)

Italicize foreign words and phrases.

> *C'est la vie* means, "That's life."

Italicize a word or phrase to add emphasis. (This should be done sparingly.)

> I said we'd be there *late*, not *at eight*.

Italicize words referred to as words, letters referred to as letters, or numbers referred to as numbers.

> The word *curfew* comes from the French. It means "cover fire" and refers to the time of day when medieval families would bank their fires and go to bed.

> Are those *0*'s, *8*'s, or *o*'s?

Hyphens

Use a hyphen to divide a word at the end of a line, if necessary. Break words only between syllables.

> splen-did
> heart-felt
> class-i-fi-ca-tion

For line breaks, divide already hyphenated words only at the hyphen.

> half-
> dollar
> many-
> sided

Use a hyphen to join two or more words serving as a single adjective before a noun.

> hand-dipped chocolates
> well-loved book

However, when compound modifiers come after a noun, they are often not hyphenated.

> The chocolates were hand dipped.
> The book was well loved.

Use a hyphen between tens and ones in compound numbers.

> twenty-seven
> one hundred forty-four

Use a hyphen with the prefixes *ex-* (meaning former), *self-*, *all-*, and *half-*, and with the suffix *-elect*.

> ex-wife
> self-critical
> all-inclusive

half-life
president-elect

Use a hyphen between a prefix and a capitalized word.

mid-October
anti-American
pre-Reformation

Use a hyphen between figures and letters.

T-shirt
mid-1900s

Dashes

En dashes (–) are used between sequential numbers, such as page ranges and date ranges.

Chapters 1–3 are due tomorrow.
The show is onstage September 20–27.

Em dashes (—) are used to set off nonrestrictive or parenthetical information or to emphasize text. Dashes can be used to show pauses or breaks in thought. They are more emphatic than commas or parentheses.

Two of the plays—*Macbeth* and *Guest by Courtesy*—are Jamie's favorites.
If you peek over the edge—watch your footing—you can see far into the canyon.
There is room in the van for six people—not 16.

Use a dash to set off an appositive phrase that already includes commas.

Three cats—Penny, Clytie, and Penguin—are in the front room.

Apostrophes

The apostrophe is used to:

- form possessives of nouns
- show the omission of letters in contractions
- indicate plurals of certain lowercase letters

Possessives of Nouns

There are several rules for making the possessive forms of nouns.

Add an apostrophe and –*s* to:

- the singular form of a word (even if it already ends in –*s*)
  a dog**'s** collar
  Mr. Rogers**'s** pocket watch
- plural forms that do not end in –*s*
  those women**'s** books
  these sheep**'s** vaccinations
- the end of compound words
  attorney-general**'s** money
  president-elect**'s** agenda
- the last name of two in a pair to show joint possession
  Ben and Max**'s** wagon
- both names in a pair to show individual possession
  Ben**'s** and Max**'s** backpacks

Add just an apostrophe to plural nouns that end in –s.

four trees' leaves
the Smiths' new house

Don't use apostrophes to make pronouns possessive or to make nouns plural.

Possessive pronouns: *his, her, hers, its, my, your, yours, our, ours, their, theirs*
Incorrect: That book is her's.
Correct: That book is **hers**.
Incorrect: Is that it's box?
Correct: Is that **its** box?
Incorrect: That book is your's.
Correct: That book is **yours**.

Contractions

Apostrophes are used in contractions to show where one or more letters or numbers have been omitted.

doesn't = does not
we're = we are
should've = should have
'70s = 1970s

Ellipses

Use ellipses, three spaced periods (…), to show where text is left out of a quoted passage.

"Four score and seven years ago our fathers brought forth on this continent, a new nation … dedicated to the proposition that all men are created equal."

Use ellipses to show a pause or break in thought.

It's just that … I don't know … maybe you're right.

Unit 1

Lesson: Parts of Speech Overview

Learning Target

- Review, identify, and use the parts of speech.

The English language is made up of words, phrases, and clauses, which in turn make up sentences. Sentences make up paragraphs, and paragraphs make up passages and larger texts. To understand English grammar, you need to understand the language's basic building blocks: parts of speech.

The term *parts of speech* refers to grammatical units, usually words (but sometimes phrases and clauses), that serve specific functions in sentences.

Common Parts of Speech and Their Functions		Examples
Noun	names a person, place, idea, thing, or animal	Owen, parrot, dragon, innocence, Eiffel Tower, light bulb
Pronoun	takes the place of one or more nouns or pronouns	I, yourself, these, which, that, most, something
Verb	expresses an action or state of being	is, be, were, hold, yank, smell, pursue
Adjective	modifies a noun or pronoun	*(boldface words are adjectives)* **a** tower, **purple** hat, **happy** face, **three** answers, **icy** river
Adverb	modifies a verb, adjective, or other adverb	*(boldface words are adverbs)* spoke **excitedly**, walked **quickly**, balanced **awkwardly**, left **beforehand**, **not** leaving
Preposition	shows the relationship of a noun or pronoun (called the object of the preposition) to another word	*(boldface words are prepositions)* spoke **to** her, walked **ahead of** Taylor, leaped **under** the beam, left **after** noon
Conjunction	joins words or word groups	and, but, or, nor, so, yet, for, either . . . or, neither . . . nor, both . . . and, because, although
Interjection	expresses emotion	whoops, oh, yay, hey, wow

Identifying Parts of Speech

Many words can function as different parts of speech. The way a word is used determines what part of speech it is.

Noun: The religious **fast** is over at sundown. *(names a thing)*

Verb: They **fast**, or refrain from eating, till sundown.

Adverb: We ran **fast**. *(modifies a verb)*

Adjective: That is a very **fast** car. *(modifies a noun)*

Check Your Understanding

Either on your own or with classmates, think of words that can be used as three or more different parts of speech. Think of at least three such words. For each word, write at least three sentences showing the word used as different parts of speech. Identify the word's part of speech in each sentence.

EXAMPLE: *oil*

Noun: My car is low on **oil**.

Verb: Did you **oil** the hinges?

Adjective: That **oil** painting is priceless.

Lesson: Verbs Overview

Learning Target
- Review and understand verb tense, voice, and mood.

Verbs are the engines that drive sentences. They tell you what *is* or what *happens*. Like engines, they have many features.

One of the most important features that verbs have is tense. **Tense** tells you when the action or state of being occurs. Here are the tenses in English:

Past: existed	**Past perfect:** had existed
Present: exist	**Present perfect:** has/have existed
Future: will exist	**Future perfect:** will have existed

Voice tells you whether the subject of the verb performs the action of the verb. If the subject performs the action, the verb is in **active voice**. In **passive voice**, the subject of the verb receives the action or is the object of the action.

Active voice: The eagle can see a mouse from hundreds of feet away. [The subject, *eagle,* performs the action of seeing.]

Passive voice: The mouse was seen from hundreds of feet away. [The subject, *mouse,* does not perform the action of seeing. It is the object of the action.]

Active voice is usually more direct and clear. In most sentences, you should use active voice.

Mood shows the mode or manner in which an action or state of being is expressed.

Mood	
indicative (facts and ordinary statements)	I **go** to baseball practice. He **was** there.
imperative (commands)	**Go** to baseball practice. **Be** there.
interrogative (questions)	**Are** you **going** to baseball practice? **Was** he there?
conditional (situations that involve certain conditions)	I **should go** to baseball practice. He **would be** there if he **could.**
subjunctive (statements about wishes or situations contrary to fact)	If I **were going** to baseball practice, I would see him. I wish I **were going.**

Check Your Understanding

Fill in the blanks with verbs in the appropriate tense, voice, and mood.

Eagles _____ much better vision than humans do. Their eyes _____ about the same size as human eyes, even though eagles themselves _____ much smaller; a full-grown bald eagle _____ only about fourteen pounds. Many eagles _____ by federal laws that make it a crime to harm endangered species. I wish I _____ an eagle. If I _____ fly like an eagle, I _____ soar through the skies and see for miles around. _____ me what kind of animal you _____ to be.

Lesson: Phrases

Learning Target
- Explain the function of phrases in general and their function in specific sentences.

In English, sentences are made of words, phrases, and clauses. A **phrase** is a word group that does NOT have both a subject and a verb and that functions as a part of speech, such as a noun or modifier (adjective or adverb). There are many different kinds of phrases. Two common kinds are prepositional phrases and appositive phrases.

Prepositional Phrases

A **preposition** is a word that shows how two or more other words relate to each other. Many prepositions show relationships involving time or location.

Common Prepositions
about, across, after, at, before, behind, below, from, in, into, like, of, out of, over, to, toward, under, upon, with, without

A **prepositional phrase** includes a preposition, a noun or pronoun that is the **object of the preposition**, and any modifiers of that object.

across the lake	at school	before dawn
below the trap door	from Jorge	in a hurry
of gold	upon a time	with justice

Prepositional phrases usually act as adjectives and adverbs. They can make writing more specific and detailed.

The house **across the lake** is empty. [The phrase acts as an adjective telling *which one*.]

A nugget **of gold** lay in the creek bed. [The phrase acts as an adjective telling *what kind*.]

The actor stands **below the trap door**. [The phrase acts as an adverb telling *where*.]

We seek those who act **with justice**. [The phrase acts as an adverb telling *how*.]

Appositive Phrases

An **appositive phrase** is a word group that acts as a noun and renames or identifies another noun or pronoun. Appositive phrases often add information to a sentence. If an appositive phrase is not necessary to the basic meaning of a sentence, it is set off with commas.

> Daniel, **my twin brother**, is getting married today. [The phrase identifies *Daniel*.]

> A long wait, **at least an hour**, came next. [The phrase adds information about *wait*.]

Check Your Understanding

Identify each boldface word group below as a *prepositional phrase* or an *appositive phrase*. Explain how the phrase functions in the sentence.

1. Benjamin, **my cousin**, likes to learn about dinosaurs.

2. That video **about dinosaurs** is his favorite.

3. Please hold that fossil **with two hands** so you don't drop it.

4. A new study, **a very interesting one**, says that many dinosaurs may have had feathers.

5. How many fossils **with feathers** have been found?

Lesson: Incorporating Quoted Text

Learning Targets

- Correctly incorporate quoted material as textual evidence in writing.
- Use an ellipsis to indicate an omission.

You will often incorporate quotations to provide **textual evidence** for your ideas.

Use quotation marks: When you are quoting directly from a text (not paraphrasing or summarizing), place the text's exact words inside quotation marks.

Frederick Douglass writes of the "wretchedness of slavery" and the "blessedness of freedom."

Place punctuation correctly: Use opening and closing quotation marks around each quoted word group. Place periods and commas inside the closing quotation marks even if they are not part of the original quotation. Place question marks and exclamation points inside the closing quotation mark only if they are part of the quotation.

In the poem, Whitman writes about Lincoln's assassination, grieving that "on the deck my Captain lies, / Fallen cold and dead."

Whitman addresses Lincoln as a leader and a parent, exclaiming "Here Captain! dear father!"

Why, in the face of the captain's death, does the speaker say "Exult O shores"?

Omitting text from a quotation: Use ellipses to show omissions from quoted text.

Douglass writes, "There I was . . . without home and without friends." [The ellipses show where words that Douglass included have been left out.]

Incorporating longer quotations: Indent quotations of more than three or four lines, and set them off without quotation marks.

Douglass writes about his sense of isolation:

> There I was in the midst of thousands, and yet a perfect stranger; without home and without friends, in the midst of thousands of my own brethren—children of a common Father, and yet I dared not to unfold to any one of them my sad condition. I was afraid to speak to anyone.

The text indicates that his loneliness was profound. . . .

Check Your Understanding

On your own paper, write three paragraphs explaining the meaning of a text or passage in your book. Use at least three quoted pieces of textual evidence to support your ideas.

Unit 2

Lesson: Punctuating Pauses, Breaks, and Omissions

Learning Targets

- Use punctuation (comma, ellipsis, dash) to indicate a pause or break.
- Use ellipses to indicate an omission.

You can use punctuation to show a pause or break in thought or speech or to show where you have left out words in a quotation.

Showing a Pause or Break in Speech

Many commas set off or separate grammatical elements in sentences. When you read, you will often interpret such a comma as a pause.

> Well, I am thinking about the problem.

For other kinds of pauses, you can use dashes and ellipses. Use an **em dash** (a long dash, as wide as an *m*, or two hyphens typed together) to show a sudden break in thought or speech:

> Anyway, we could alphabetize the files and—are you even listening?

> When you get to the corner you'll turn—hey, watch out for that cyclist!

Use **ellipses** (three spaced periods) to show thought or speech trailing off or pausing:

> I'm not sure I know the . . . um, could you repeat the question?

If the pause is at the end of a complete sentence or between two complete sentences, you should use the ellipses AND correct end punctuation for each sentence.

> Let me think about it. . . . Honestly, I don't think it will work.

Showing an Omission

When you are quoting someone else, you can use ellipses to show where you have left out words. For instance, if the person you are quoting said, "The poet uses several figures of speech, including similes and metaphors, to compare the mountain to a giant," and you want to leave out *including similes and metaphors,* you would use three spaced periods to show the omission:

"The poet uses several figures of speech . . . to compare the mountain to a giant."

Check Your Understanding

A. On your own paper, write a short dialogue between two people who are trying to figure something out or solve a problem. Use at least two ellipses to show pauses in speech or a speaker trailing off. Also use two dashes to show breaks in thought or speech.

B. On your own paper, write down a long quotation. Then, rewrite it, omitting some words and using ellipses to show where the omissions are. Make sure the quotation still makes sense.

Lesson: Active and Passive Voice

Learning Targets
- Form and use verbs in the active and passive voice.
- Recognize and correct inappropriate shifts in verb voice.
- Use verbs in the active and passive voice to achieve particular effects (e.g., emphasizing the actor or the action).

Active and Passive Voice

Voice tells you whether the subject of the verb performs or receives the action of the verb. If the subject performs the action, the verb is in **active voice**. In **passive voice**, the subject of the verb receives the action or is the object of the action.

> **Active voice:** The squirrel **buries** a pecan. [The subject, *squirrel,* performs the action of burying.]

> **Passive voice:** The pecan **is buried** by the squirrel. [The subject, *pecan,* does not perform the action of burying. It is the object of the action, which means that it receives the action.]

A verb in the passive voice includes a form of the verb *be*, a past participle of a verb, and any needed helping verbs.

Tense	Examples of Passive Voice
Present	The pecan **is buried.** The pecans **are buried.**
Past	The pecan **was buried.** The pecans **were buried.**
Future	The pecan (or pecans) **will be buried.**
Present Perfect	The pecan **has been buried.** The pecans **have been buried.**
Past Perfect	The (pecan or pecans) **had been buried.**
Future Perfect	The pecan (or pecans) **will have been buried.**

Active voice is usually more direct and clear. In most sentences, you should use active voice. However, you may use passive voice when you want to emphasize the action or the recipient of the action, or when you do not know who performed the action. You may also use passive voice to avoid pointing fingers or naming names.

Active voice: John Smith **made** several mistakes.

Passive voice: Several mistakes **were made.**

Use the voice that best achieves your purpose with the fewest words. Do not shift between active and passive voice unnecessarily.

Unnecessary shift: We **worked** in the yard, and several bags of leaves **were raked up.**

Better: We **worked** in the yard and **raked up** several bags of leaves.

Check Your Understanding

Revise the following sentences, changing passive voice verbs to active voice verbs.

EXAMPLE: The trees were climbed by Max and Ben.

Max and Ben **climbed** the trees.

1. The main dish was made by Olivia.

2. The virus will have been detected by my computer by then.

3. Our cat has been chased by the neighbor's dog.

4. The fog was produced by rapidly warming temperatures and high humidity.

5. Several assignments were missed by Gavin when he was out sick.

Lesson: Mood

Learning Targets

- Recognize and correct inappropriate shifts in verb mood.
- Use verbs in the conditional and subjunctive mood to achieve particular effects (e.g., expressing uncertainty or describing a state contrary to fact).

Verbs

Verbs express being or action. A verb tells you what *is* or what *happens,* and it is one of the most important parts of a sentence. Verbs have tense, voice, and mood. In this lesson, we will be exploring mood.

Mood shows the mode or manner in which an action or state of being is expressed. You should use mood appropriately, avoiding unnecessary shifts. However, varying mood wisely and purposefully can create specific effects and enliven your writing.

For instance, when you are writing for school, you will mostly use indicative mood. However, you can use interrogative mood or imperative mood to catch the reader's attention by asking a question, giving a command, or making a request.

You can also use conditional mood to express actions that depend on certain conditions or subjunctive to express wishes or situations contrary to fact.

Mood	Examples
indicative (facts and ordinary statements)	Taylor **plays** saxophone. She **practices** every day.
imperative (commands)	**Play** saxophone. **Practice** every day.
interrogative (questions)	**Will** you **play** saxophone? **Do** you **practice** every day?
conditional (situations that involve certain conditions)	I **should play** an instrument. I **would like** to play the trumpet.
subjunctive (statements about wishes or situations contrary to fact)	If I **were playing** in the band, I would play the trumpet. I wish I **were** in the band.

Check Your Understanding

Fill in the blanks with verbs or helping verbs in an appropriate mood.

(1) _____ me a story, please.

What kinds of stories (2) _____ you (3) _____?

My favorite stories (4) _____ myths and folktales.

If I (5) _____ a writer, I (6) _____ try to write imaginative short stories.

(7) _____ it true that every culture (8) _____ made-up stories?

I wish I (9) _____ a character in *The Thousand and One Nights*.

(10) _____ you like to go back in time?

Unit 3

Lesson: Participles and Participial Phrases

Learning Target

- Explain the function of verbals, such as participles, in general and their function in particular sentences.

A **phrase** is a word group that does NOT have both a subject and a verb and that functions as a part of speech, such as a noun or modifier (adjective or adverb). There are different kinds of phrases. You can enliven your writing by using phrases to vary your syntax and add detail.

A **verbal** is a verb form that is used as a noun, adjective, or adverb. Verbals include *infinitives, participles,* and *gerunds.* A **verbal phrase** is a word group that contains a verbal and its modifiers and complements and that acts as a noun, adjective, or adverb. This mini-lesson focuses on participles and participial phrases.

Participle and Participial Phrases

A **participle** is a verb form that can be used as an adjective. Present participles end in *–ing.* Past participles often end in *–ed.*

> A **singing** bird is outside my window. [The participle modifies *bird*.]

> The **buried** treasure includes gold doubloons. [The participle modifies *treasure*.]

A **participial phrase** includes a participle and any modifiers or objects of the participle.

> The bird <u>**singing** outside my window</u> is a mockingbird. [The phrase modifies *bird*.]

> The treasure <u>**buried** by Spanish pirates</u> includes gold doubloons. [The phrase modifies *treasure*.]

If a participial phrase is not essential to the meaning of the sentence—if it adds extra information without changing the sentence's basic meaning—it should be set off by commas.

> Elaine, <u>**worrying** about the weather,</u> suggested we cancel the picnic.

> <u>**Playing** for the first time ever,</u> Ethan won the game.

Check Your Understanding

Revise each of the following sentences by including at least two participles or participial phrases to add detail and make the sentences more interesting. You may reword the sentences to add some phrases. Underline each participle and participial phrase.

1. The vine grew well.

2. The cliff was mostly limestone.

3. Brenner saw a spider on the flower pot.

4. Benjamin crossed to the other side of the river.

5. The glasses were behind the bookshelves.

Lesson: Clauses

Learning Target

- Use different types of clauses to convey specific meanings and add variety and interest to writing.

Sentences are made of clauses. **Clauses** contain subjects and verbs and may contain modifiers, objects, complements, and other sentence parts. Different kinds of sentences contain different numbers and kinds of clauses. You can use various kinds of clauses to express different relationships among ideas, to create a more mature style, and to increase reader or listener interest.

An **independent clause** contains a subject and a verb and expresses a complete thought. It can stand alone as a complete sentence.

> **EXAMPLE:** This is an independent clause.

A **dependent** (or **subordinate**) **clause** contains a subject and a verb but does not express a complete thought. It cannot stand alone as a complete sentence.

> **EXAMPLE:** because this is a dependent clause

There are different kinds of dependent clauses. Using a variety of dependent clauses can enliven your writing and help you vary syntax.

A **noun clause** can act as a subject, object, appositive, or any other sentence part that a one-word noun can.

> **What you see** is **what you get.** [*What you see* is the subject of the sentence. *What you get* is a predicate nominative.]

> I don't know **whether the train is late**. [*Whether the train is late* is the object of the verb *know*.]

An **adjectival clause** (often called a **relative clause**) acts as a modifier of a noun or pronoun.

> The paint set **that he donated** is very nice. [The clause modifies *paint set*.]

An **adverbial clause** acts as a modifier of a verb, adjective, or other adverb.

> **Although we thought we left early enough,** we still didn't get there in time. [The clause modifies the verb *did get*.]

> Hungry **even though we had had a big lunch,** Trevor asked for a snack. [The clause modifies the adjective *hungry*.]

Check Your Understanding

A. For each of the following five sentences, identify each of the boldface clauses, and label it *independent* or *dependent*. If the clause is dependent, tell whether it is a *noun clause, adjectival (relative) clause,* or *adverbial clause.*

1. **After Tristan woke up,** he went to the kitchen for breakfast.

2. The house **that is on the corner** belongs to Nikki.

3. Ellie has a pet frog, and **Diego has a dog.**

4. **What I heard** is that rehearsal has been canceled.

5. The ice chest, **which is full of ice and water,** is too heavy for me to carry.

B. Write a simple sentence, with just one subject and one verb: an independent clause. Then rewrite that sentence, adding at least one adjectival clause. Rewrite the new sentence, adding at least one adverbial clause. Finally, rewrite the sentence to include at least one noun clause. Underline and identify the clauses as shown in the example.

    EXAMPLE

    Simple sentence (independent clause): We watched a movie.

    With adjectival clause: We watched a movie <u>that was about an orphan</u>.

    With adverbial clause: <u>After we got home</u>, we watched a movie <u>that was about an orphan</u>.

    With noun clause: <u>After we got home</u> from <u>where we spent the afternoon</u>, we watched a movie <u>that was about an orphan</u>.

Lesson: Commas with Nonessential Elements

Learning Target

- Use commas correctly to set off nonessential elements.

Commas are used to set off certain nonessential grammatical elements, such as nonrestrictive appositives, interrupting elements, and introductory elements.

Nonrestrictive Appositives and Appositive Phrases

If an appositive or appositive phrase is **nonrestrictive** (that is, not essential to the basic meaning of the sentence), it is set off with commas. If leaving out the appositive or appositive phrase would change the meaning of the sentence, it is not set off.

> The American author **Madeleine L'Engle** wrote *A Wrinkle in Time*. [The appositive *Madeleine L' Engle* is essential to the basic meaning of the sentence. It **restricts** the meaning of author. Without the appositive, the reader does not know which American author is meant.]

> Madeleine L'Engle, **an American author,** wrote *A Wrinkle in Time*. [The appositive *an American author* adds extra information; it is nonessential.]

Interrupting Elements

Nouns of **direct address** are set off:

> **Isabelle,** have you read *A Swiftly Tilting Planet*?

> Have you read *A Swiftly Tilting Planet*, **Isabelle**?

Parenthetical expressions are usually set off:

> **By the way,** that's my favorite book.

> The books, **as I recall,** include interesting ideas about time travel.

Introductory Elements

When *yes, no, well,* or a **mild interjection** begins a sentence, it is set off with a comma:

> **Yes,** I have read that book. **Boy,** did I love it!

When a **long prepositional phrase** or a **series of two or more short prepositional phrases** begins a sentence, it is set off with a comma:

> **Of all the books that you have read this year,** which is your favorite?

> **In the library at our school,** there is a book that I have read at least five times.

When **an adverb clause** begins a sentence, it is set off with a comma:

> **When I read,** it is as if I am visiting another world.

> **Because the library is closed on Thursday,** we plan to go on Friday.

Other Nonessential Elements

Nonessential participial phrases (those that add information that is not necessary to the basic meaning of the sentence) are set off with commas:

> **Sitting down to Thanksgiving dinner,** Meg's family learns of a serious threat to the world.

> Charles Wallace, **reciting an ancient Irish rune,** summons the unicorn Gaudior.

Nonessential adjectival clauses are set off with commas:

> Meg's family, **who are sitting down to Thanksgiving dinner,** learns of a serious threat to the world.

> Charles Wallace, **who recites an ancient Irish rune,** summons the unicorn Gaudior.

Check Your Understanding

Read the following sentences. Add any missing commas. If a sentence is already correct as is, write *Correct*.

1. We have had our boat a sixteen-foot aluminum canoe for over twenty years.

2. On the surface of the bay you can sometimes see fish jumping.

3. There's a particular kind of fish the mullet that frequently jumps out of the water.

4. Standing on the pier Walter saw a jellyfish.

5. Although we applied sunscreen we still got a little sunburned.

6. Did you see the jetty Chris?

7. Yes we walked there yesterday.

8. Watching the sunset Frank saw a flock of pelicans fly overhead.

9. My friend Eliana likes stargazing.

10. By the way I hope we get to camp on the beach.

Unit 4

Lesson: Verbals and Verbal Phrases

Learning Target

• Explain the function of verbals (gerunds, participles, infinitives) in general and their function in particular sentences.

Verbals and Verbal Phrases

A **phrase** is a word group that does NOT have both a subject and a verb and that functions as a part of speech, such as a noun or modifier (adjective or adverb). There are many different kinds of phrases. You can enliven your writing by using phrases to vary your syntax and add detail.

A **verbal** is a verb form that is used as a noun, adjective, or adverb. A **verbal phrase** is a word group that contains a verbal and its modifiers and complements and that acts as a noun, adjective, or adverb.

A **participle** is a verb form, often ending in –*ing,* that can be used as an adjective. A **participial phrase** includes a participle and any modifiers or objects of the participle.

There are eight planets **revolving around the sun**. [The phrase modifies *planets.*]

Casting a silvery light, the stars glow brightly tonight. [The phrase modifies *stars.*]

A **gerund** is a verb form ending in –*ing* that is used as a noun. A **gerund phrase** includes a gerund and any modifiers or objects of the gerund.

The **twinkling** of stars is caused by the **passing of light** through different layers of an atmosphere in motion. [*The twinkling of stars* is a gerund phrase acting as the subject of the sentence. The gerund phrase *the passing of light* is the object of the preposition *by.*]

An **infinitive** is a verb form that is preceded by *to* and that can be used as a noun, adjective, or adverb. An **infinitive phrase** includes an infinitive and any modifiers or objects of the infinitive.

To study astronomy is my goal. [The phrase is a noun that is the subject of the sentence.]

We will use a telescope **to see the rings of Saturn**. [The phrase is an adverb modifying *will use.*]

Subjects **to study** include galaxies and our solar system. [The phrase is an adjective that modifies *subjects.*]

Check Your Understanding

Identify each boldface word group below as a *participial phrase*, a *gerund phrase*, or an *infinitive phrase*. Then say whether it functions as a *noun, adjective,* or *adverb.*

1. **Shaking with laughter,** Jack replayed the video.

2. Are you willing **to help out at the fundraiser**?

3. **Going to the store** should take less than an hour.

4. The hummingbirds **flying around the garden** are beautiful.

5. Let's find something **to wedge under the short table leg**.

Lesson: Pronoun–Antecedent Agreement

Learning Target
- Demonstrate command of the conventions of standard English grammar and usage when writing or speaking.

Pronoun–Antecedent Agreement

Pronouns are words that take the place of nouns or other pronouns and refer to people, places, things, and ideas. The words they take the place of or refer to are called the pronouns' **antecedents.** Pronouns should **agree with** (have the same gender and number as) their antecedents. Pronouns can be **masculine** (and refer to male persons or animals), **feminine** (and refer to female persons or animals), or **neuter** (and refer to things or to people or animals of unspecified gender).

Each **boy** should have **his** calendar. [The pronoun *his* refers to the antecedent *boy*. Both the pronoun and its antecedent are singular and masculine, so they agree.]

Each **girl** should have **her** calendar. [The pronoun *her* refers to the antecedent *girl*. Both the pronoun and its antecedent are singular and feminine, so they agree.]

All **students** should have **their** calendars. [The pronoun *their* refers to the antecedent *students*. Both the pronoun and its antecedent are plural and neuter, so they agree.]

Clear Reference

Make sure that it is clear whom or what a pronoun refers to. Sometimes you will need to rewrite a sentence to make the sentence clear.

Unclear: After Ms. Cox talked to Angelica, she decided to try out a new idea. [Who decided?]

Clear: Ms. Cox decided to try out a new idea after **she** talked to Angelica.

Clear: Angelica decided to try out a new idea after **she** talked to Ms. Cox.

Unclear: Trevor makes beautiful artwork. They are amazing. [What does *they* refer to?]

Clear: Trevor makes amazing, beautiful artwork.

Clear: Trevor is amazing; he makes beautiful artwork.

Check Your Understanding

For items 1–4, fill in the blank with a correct pronoun form.

EXAMPLE: The co-chairs are Cyndi and Miriam. Have you met _them_ ?

1. All of the students who are auditioning should bring _____ scripts.

2. Please ask Jeremy or Justin to lend us _____ pencil for a minute.

3. Stella or Ava has _____ answer ready.

4. My neighbor has chickens named Olive and Dodger. Would you like to see _____?

For item 5, rewrite the sentence to correct the unclear pronoun reference.

5. Are the boys still going to meet with Marcy and Katelyn, or have they already left?

Lesson: Apostrophes

Learning Target

- Demonstrate command of the conventions of standard English punctuation.

Apostrophes are punctuation marks that are used to form contractions and to indicate possession.

Contractions

A **contraction** is a shortened form of a word, word group, or number. An apostrophe takes the place of any letters or numbers that have been left out.

cannot can't   I am I'm

of the clock o'clock   1950s '50s

Possessives

Use an apostrophe to form the possessive case of nouns.

Singular nouns usually take an apostrophe and an –s:

class's library

the cat's toy

Plural nouns ending in –s usually take just an apostrophe:

classes' libraries

those cats' toys

Many irregular plural nouns take an apostrophe and an –s:

sheep's pasture

children's playground

Use an apostrophe to form the possessive case of indefinite pronouns (pronouns that don't refer to specific persons).

anyone's time

everybody's effort

Do NOT use an apostrophe to form the possessive case of personal pronouns (pronouns that refer to specific persons).

Incorrect: That notebook is your's.

Correct: That notebook is **yours**.

Incorrect: It's hinge is rusted.

Correct: Its hinge is rusted.

Plurals

There are very few instances when you should use an apostrophe to form a plural:

lowercase letters: four *s*'s in *Mississippi*

some capital letters: two *A*'s not written clearly

many numbers and symbols: several *1*'s, *7*'s, and *0*'s, as well as *!*'s, *#*'s, and */*'s

words referred to as words: How many *Mississippi*'s did you count?

These apostrophes are generally necessary to prevent misreading. For instance, in "two *A*'s," the expression might seem to include the word *As* if it did not include an apostrophe.

Most of the time, though, you should not use an apostrophe to form a plural:

Incorrect: two Sunday's in a row

Correct: two **Sundays** in a row

Incorrect: many apostrophe's on the page

Correct: many **apostrophes** on the page

Check Your Understanding

Read the following sentences. Add any missing apostrophes. Delete any extra apostrophes. If a sentence is already correct as is, write *Correct.*

1. It's true that they have lived here for seventeen year's.
2. I cant decide whether the dog or its owner is nicer.
3. How many *i*s are in the word *mischievous*?
4.   In the 80s we listened to a lot of British electronic music.
5. Is it everyones understanding that we are second on the program?
6. The womens' room is downstairs.
7. How many pairs of glasses are on Dr. Smith's shelf?
8. Look at all those blue jay's!
9. My friend Paul like's stargazing; its his favorite pastime.
10. Your essay contains several *however*'s.

Notes